Calculated Risk

A Provider's Guide to Assessing and Controlling the Financial Risk of Managed Care

Bruce S. Pyenson, FSA, MAAA, Editor
Milliman & Robertson, Inc.

AHA books are published by
American Hospital Publishing, Inc.,
an American Hospital Association company

Although this publication is designed to provide accurate and authoritative information in regard to the subject matter covered, it is sold with the understanding that the publisher is not engaged in rendering legal, accounting, actuarial, or other professional service. If legal, actuarial, or other expert advice or assistance is required, the services of a competent professional person should be sought.

The views expressed in this publication are strictly those of the authors and do not necessarily represent official positions of the American Hospital Association.

Library of Congress Cataloging-in-Publication Data

Calculated risk : a provider's guide to assessing and controlling the
    financial risk of managed care / Bruce S. Pyenson, editor.
        p.   cm. — (Tools for change)
    Includes bibliographical references.
    ISBN 1-55648-131-4
    1. Health facilities—Risk management—United States.   2. Managed
care plans (Medical care)—United States.   3. Health facilities—
United States—Business management.   I. Pyenson, Bruce.
II. Series.
    [DNLM: 1. Managed Care Programs—organization & administration—
United States.   2. Delivery of Health Care—economics—United
States.   3. Risk.   4. Risk Management—organization &
administration.   W 130 C144 1995]
RA971.38.C35 1995
362.1'068'1—dc20
for Library of Congress   94-47276
                                                                                                        CIP

Catalog no. 131001

Printed in the USA

𝔸ℍ𝔸 is a service mark of the American Hospital Association used under license by American Hospital Publishing, Inc.

Text set in Times
10M—2/95—0399

Anne Hermann, Editor
Peggy DuMais, Production Coordinator
Luke Smith, Cover Designer
Marcia Bottoms, Executive Editor
Brian Schenk, Director

Contents

About the Authors

Milliman & Robertson, Inc., is an international firm of consultants and actuaries with offices in major cities throughout the United States. With almost 1,000 employees, M&R uses actuarial risk management expertise to provide strategic and tactical advice to a full range of financial and health care organizations, providers, governments, and employers. The firm has helped many HMOs, insurance companies, Blue Cross/Blue Shield Plans, and providers measure their financial status, appraise business opportunities, develop new products, and determine premium rates. We are pleased to work with the American Hospital Association to publish this document.

Note: In the following credits, FSA stands for Fellow of the Society of Actuaries, the highest designation given by the Society of Actuaries, which is the examination and education body for the majority of actuaries specializing in health care; ASA stands for Associate of the Society of Actuaries; and MAAA stands for Member of the American Academy of Actuaries. The AAA is the umbrella organization for various actuarial bodies in the U.S. and functions as the liaison between the actuarial profession and government regulators.

Bruce S. Pyenson, FSA, MAAA, is a consulting actuary in M&R's New York City office. Mr. Pyenson has consulted to a wide variety of providers, medical suppliers, HMOs, and insurers on issues ranging from health care reform to capitation development. His time with M&R includes a year spent in the United Kingdom where he consulted to the growing private health care sector.

David V. Axene, FSA, MAAA, is a consulting actuary in M&R's Seattle office. He is well known for his work with Dr. Richard L. Doyle in developing methods for integrating actuarial science and medicine so that managed care organizations can determine how clinical practice affects financial goals.

Richard L. Doyle, M.D., is a senior health care consultant in M&R's San Diego office and author of M&R's *Healthcare Management Guidelines,* a collection of medical protocols that have been widely adopted by managed care organizations. Working with author David Axene, Dr. Doyle has developed methods for integrating actuarial science and medicine. Prior to becoming M&R's first physician consultant in 1989, Dr. Doyle was clinical director for a large San Diego multispecialty practice and was active in managed care organizations.

Greg N. Herrle, FSA, MAAA, is a consulting actuary in M&R's Milwaukee office. Mr. Herrle has consulted on managed care issues to a wide range of HMOs, PHOs, physician organizations, and insurance companies.

Timothy D. Lee, FSA, MAAA, is a consulting actuary based in M&R's Houston office. Mr. Lee has consulted to many HMOs and insurers, and has been heavily involved in PHO development.

Howard A. Levin, M.D., is a senior consultant in M&R's Philadelphia office. Prior to joining M&R, Dr. Levin spent seven years as a medical director at US Healthcare where he directed a variety of operations ranging from physician recruitment to developing report cards on physician efficiency. He also has 14 years' managing and practicing experience at a California multispecialty group.

Oscar M. Lucas, ASA, MAAA, is a senior consultant in M&R's Seattle office. Mr. Lucas has an extensive background in managed care.

David G. Ogden, FSA, MAAA, is a consulting actuary in M&R's Milwaukee office. Mr. Ogden has consulted on managed care issues to a wide range of HMOs, PHOs, hospitals, and insurance companies.

M&R consultants other than the individual chapter authors who provided valuable advice in the preparation of this publication include: Drew Davidoff, FSA; Bob Dymowski, FSA; Marlese Pinney, R.N.; Fred Spong, M.D.; and Art Wilmes, FSA. The editor would also like to acknowledge the encouragement of all the health care consultants at M&R who in one way or another supported this project.

The publisher wishes to acknowledge the advice and contributions during the development of this publication of Donna Melkonian, senior director, AHA Tools for Change Initiative; John Fry, director, clinical service contracting, University of Utah School of Medicine; and Lynn Simons, a Salt Lake City-based independent consultant.

Introduction

Risk and Health Care Integration

The move to integrated delivery networks and the continued growth of managed care have deepened health care providers' interest in assuming financial risk for the cost of care. Indeed, how providers respond to the new risk-sharing arrangements will help determine:

- How hospitals will manage the overcapacity challenge
- Whether providers—hospitals, physicians, and others—can create successful integrated delivery networks
- Whether providers can successfully partner with managed care organizations and insurers

Developing integrated networks and successfully managing capitated arrangements will require provider risk management functions similar to those that insurers and managed care organizations have used. The authors will demonstrate that successful financial risk management functions depend on a broad array of health care management functions, including:

- Controlling and allocating variable and fixed costs
- Managing how care is delivered and by whom
- Marketing health care services to buyers who are pitting sellers against one another to reduce costs
- Complying with health care financing regulations

To the extent that providers assume these functions, they assume at least some of the functions of insurers. For hospitals, in particular, the assumption of insurerlike functions will drive evolution in every aspect of their operations and in every department.

However, creating integrated delivery networks is not the only motivation for providers to learn more about assuming and managing risk. A number of managed care organizations have succeeded by using strategies that shift risk to fragmented providers. These payers have built networks by contracting directly with individual general practitioners, specialists, general hospitals, psychiatric hospitals, tertiary hospitals, ancillary providers, prescription services, and other providers.

Can a provider succeed as a specialist in a nonintegrated system? Does a given provider have to form or join an integrated delivery network to succeed? The answers to these questions depend on the local/regional health care market, the interests and capabilities of the provider and its partners, and the actions of buyers in the market. This publication outlines steps to help providers develop risk management strategies wherever the providers lie along the continuum from specialization to fully integrated networks.

Aspects of Risk

This publication concentrates on the provider's financial risk as it relates to payment for health care. New risk-sharing arrangements (such as capitation) are the focus because the amount paid for any given individual's package of services will not match the provider's cost for providing that individual's services.

In addition to surveying the nature of a provider's financial risk, this publication presents tools that health care executives can use to manage the new risk-sharing arrangements:

- *Analytical:* To measure past performance, estimate risk, and project probable results
- *Financial:* To manage key incentive and risk protection issues
- *Clinical/operational:* To manage health care delivery and resource use
- *Administrative:* To manage marketing and underwriting functions and assess their roles in risk

Providers must not ignore solvency and capital issues, such as the capital that may be required to handle unexpected costs. Additionally, HMOs and insurers are prompting state insurance departments to extend their regulatory reach to risk-taking providers.

This publication does not address risk issues such as employee benefits, malpractice, property, or liability, although providers will want to assess their ability to manage these risks as well. Additionally, it is not designed to be a "cookbook" to developing an integrated, risk-bearing system. Providers should develop or seek competent design, legal, medical, and actuarial assistance once they decide to integrate.

Why Assume Risk?

In general, hospitals and other health care providers assume risk in order to support their purpose—the delivery of health care. By contrast, insurance companies assume risk as their core business. Increasingly, however, some providers are merging the delivery and risk assumption associated with health care.

As chapters 1, 3, and 6 explain, payers want providers to assume financial risk because:

- Managed care organizations and insurers can limit their own financial risk by contracting with providers to accept some of that risk.
- Payers who place risk with health care providers move potential profits (and losses) closer to the only groups that can truly deliver (or fail to deliver) efficiency. Well-designed incentives may reduce the payer's need for expensive cost-control efforts.

For their part, providers may want to assume risk because:

- It offers a bargaining chip (perhaps in addition to discounts and scope or quality of services) to win sophisticated customers.
- Providers obtain financial rewards if they manage risk well.
- Providers may avoid some "middleman" functions of insurance companies.
- It enhances local control of the delivery and quality of health care services.
- It may "lock in" a base of patients.

The external forces causing providers to assume risk can dramatically change how providers measure internal success. Though an oversimplification, under traditional fee-for-service arrangements, the more health care resources a provider employs, the more it succeeds. Under many of the new financial arrangements, providers succeed if they deliver quality care using appropriate levels of resources.

For example, under traditional arrangements, an endocrinologist with a high volume of diabetic admissions brings income to the hospital. Under capitation arrangements, such an endocrinologist potentially loses money for the hospital or integrated network compared with one who brings about healthy patient life-styles and treats patients effectively outside the hospital. As this example suggests, the new risk-sharing arrangements are about something more than profit and loss. They also provide incentives to promote quality improvement initiatives, as well as health promotion or community health benefit programs.

Chapter 1

What Are Managed Care Risks?

Bruce S. Pyenson, FSA, MAAA

The New Elements of Provider Risk

Like other businesses, health care providers face many kinds of risks and often these risks are interrelated. Additionally, the risks faced by health care providers today contain new elements. For the purposes of this publication, the new elements of provider risk fall into three categories:

- *Underpricing:* Expenses are greater than revenue because the prices charged are too low. Underpricing is not a new risk, but the new environment requires new approaches to forecasting and managing revenue and expenses.
- *Fluctuation:* This refers to random, "unlucky," or infrequent events such as a run of premature babies or transplants in a risk pool. Many people associate this kind of risk with Lloyds of London. Health care executives may be particularly concerned about fluctuation—especially if they are also worried about underpricing.
- *Business:* New kinds of business risk arise from the risk-sharing arrangement, including managing and distributing capitation payments, collecting required copayments, and assessing the financial stability of partners.

Although providers face other new risks, such as regulators constraining the kinds of businesses a provider can enter, this chapter concentrates on the basic issues.

Underpricing Risk

How much should a provider charge for a particular service? How much should it charge for all the services 100,000 people will need in one month?

Underpricing risk is the danger that the provider will charge too little. Similarly, overpricing can mean the provider will become uncompetitive.

The commonsense idea that a company gets into trouble if revenue is less than its expenses is made more complex by new risk arrangements. For example, a hospital may agree to an HMO's per diem reimbursement because it believes that the per diem will generate sufficient revenue. However, if the HMO's physicians reduce patient length of stay (LOS), reimbursement may decrease more than the hospital's expenses and the hospital could lose money on this group of patients. This will happen unless the hospital becomes more efficient, because the days that are not eliminated—the first days of the stay—are the most expensive for the hospital. (Strategies to address this phenomenon are discussed in chapter 3.)

Underpricing risk also occurs when hospitals and other providers charge HMOs marginal rates. Such rates may cover the cost of providing services to an additional volume of patients, given the total current patient volume, but may not cover the average cost of all patients. Expenses include fixed and variable components; marginal pricing may cover all or a major part of the variable portion but little or none of the fixed portion. This practice can lead to a downward pricing spiral as follows:

1. The HMO's lower marginal cost may give it a significant cost advantage.
2. This cost advantage allows the HMO to sell its products at lower premium rates, attracting more members.
3. The HMO's larger enrollment and volume of business gives it leverage to demand larger discounts from the hospital.
4. The HMO has an even greater cost advantage, and the cycle continues.

If the provider's own costs do not decrease, the cycle may cause the hospital to lose money under the HMO contract. Underpricing risk clearly causes more complexity for the provider. No longer can expense be grossly identified and a simple margin added.

Fluctuation Risk

Some people call fluctuation risks "insurance risks" because these are the kinds of risk they associate with insurance companies (for example, a homeowner's insurance protection against the unlikely occurrence of a fire).

Random risk ("Bad things happen") occurs on both a large scale (such as epidemics) and a small scale (such as an unusually high number of heart transplants). Aside from these examples, fluctuation risk also includes the cases when a normally simple procedure goes awry and expensive complications set in.

Following are examples of fluctuation risks:

- *Epidemics:* Death rates soared during the 1918 influenza epidemic. If such an epidemic were to occur again, the medical costs could be enormous. Would insurers, HMOs, or capitated hospitals become insolvent? All the chapters in this publication address some of the issues related to this risk, especially chapters 2 and 3.

- *Coincidence:* In 1993, there were two heart transplants among the 2,000 people covered by the authors' firm's health benefits program, which was about 20 times the national average rate of 5 per 100,000 people for the under-65 population. Was this coincidence, or is the group a bad risk? Who bore the loss? Chapter 3 examines this issue and discusses stop-loss insurance.
- *Severity:* Cholecystectomies are fairly routine operations, with a national average LOS of somewhat more than three days. However, in rare instances something goes wrong and the patient stays for a month. If this patient were a Medicare DRG patient, his or her LOS would cause the hospital to lose a lot of money. Are events like this random, or are they associated with improvable physician practices? Chapters 2, 3, and 5 provide some strategies for reducing the likelihood of risk: Chapter 2 discusses the importance of evaluating what kinds of risk the provider may be absorbing, chapter 3 discusses stop-loss insurance, and chapter 5 discusses how quality and efficiency are parallel.

Fluctuation risks become much more dangerous financially if the provider has underpriced its product or faces unusual business risks.

Business and Administrative Risk

Business risk is not new, but in the changing environment, there are many new forms and health system management has new responsibilities. Following are a few examples of this risk.

Capitation Management

Capitation management is a new risk for integrated systems. Providers are paid per covered member and must carefully track enrollment to ensure that all patients who might receive care are being paid for. Capitation distribution must also be fair and auditable to ensure hospitals, physicians, and others receive appropriate portions of revenue and profit.

Copay Collection

Suppose an HMO contracts with a hospital for a $1,000 medical/surgical per diem, but the *hospital* must collect a $500 per admission patient copay. The $1,000 per diem charge may be adequate, but if the hospital does not develop the administrative systems to bill and collect the patient-pay portion, the contract could lead to large losses.

Financial Stability and Legitimacy of Partners

Like other businesses, managed care organizations and insurers can become insolvent. Payer financial and systems problems can lead to delayed and uncertain payments. In many cases, systems problems result from (or are related to) financial problems. Furthermore, most HMO contracts with providers contain hold-harmless provisions that prevent the provider from collecting bills from patients in the event of HMO insolvency.

Entrepreneurs and existing organizations are creating new kinds of provider, marketing, risk-taking, and payer ventures. Sponsors of these ventures may include: (1) health care providers such as physician group practices, medical societies, and hospitals; (2) insurance agents or brokers; (3) third-party administrators; (4) insurance companies; (5) HMOs or PPOs; and (6) venture capitalists. These entrepreneurs and organizations may bring important pieces of the health care market and important skills to health care networks. Nevertheless, management should ask these difficult questions before entering into a contractual relationship:

- Does the venture have sufficient capital to cover start-up costs? What is sufficient capital?
- Can the venture actually deliver the promised volume of patients and revenue?
- Can the venture actuarially demonstrate that promised cost advantages are likely to materialize?
- Does the venture have all necessary regulatory approvals or a plan to obtain such approvals? What is the impact of a regulatory decision that the venture is really an insurance company or HMO and must be licensed?
- What do the partners bring in terms of skills, market and political connections, capital, and so on? What makes their proposal better than competing proposals—or the status quo?
- Does the proposed arrangement enhance the delivery of high-quality, efficient services?

The Changing Nature of Health Care Risk

Insurers, managed care organizations, and employers who once assumed health care risk today are contractually shifting that risk to hospitals and other health care providers. Shifting risk to providers also helps insurers and managed care organizations lower the costs they pass on to buyers. A major driving force for shifting risk is the *cost* of health services, despite the fact that by late 1994, the double-digit increases in health care costs subsided dramatically. With health benefits costing approximately $4,000 per employee (as calculated by Milliman

& Robertson through its 1994 *Health Cost Guidelines*), employers often flock to insurers or HMOs that offer lower costs.

In most areas of the country, managed care organizations and insurers have gained a competitive advantage because they have bargained with hospitals and other providers for lower costs. Hospitals, physicians, and other providers are often vulnerable to aggressive bargaining because they have excess capacity.

A basic issue confronting both payers and providers is how to manage costs by improving the management of patient care. Payers traditionally focused on simple systems such as fee schedules and second-opinion requirements and sophisticated approaches to utilization management. Because the real cost of care is in the hands of providers, many of these programs have had limited impact on the way resources are used. Now the efficiency and effectiveness of providers are being probed more deeply, as for example, through quality initiatives such as total quality management (TQM) and continuous quality improvement (CQI).

New contractual arrangements focusing provider attention on cost present threats to providers. Providers should be aware of the following:

- Accepting DRG-based schedules, per diems, or discounts that guarantee a loss even when costs are adequately controlled.
- Not knowing how to manage the deal. For example, a capitated general hospital may have obligated itself to provide behavioral health services but may have no specialized knowledge of managing psychiatric diagnoses.
- Not being able to rapidly restructure care delivery. For example, a hospital being paid under a DRG-based system may face operational or financial problems when it tries to reduce costs by shifting from inpatient to home care delivery of a service.
- Not having control over health care management. For example, a hospital paid under capitation or DRGs may be at risk if there are ineffective incentives for the HMO physicians to reduce LOS.

These risks to providers are discussed further in chapter 3.

Provider Adaptation of Insurer Functions

As financial risk takers, insurance companies perform many functions outside the usual repertoire of hospitals and other health care providers. As health care providers assume risk, they need to see the parallels between these functions and the changes they will need to make. Certainly, integrated delivery networks may have to perform some or all of the following functions:

- Assume, finance, and manage risk
- Underwrite and select risk
- Sell and market integrated services and products
- Administer bills, claims, premiums, enrollment, eligibility
- Deal with insurance regulators
- Manage appropriate levels and amounts of care

Chapter 6 explores these functions in more detail.

How Is Risk Measured and Evaluated?

David V. Axene, FSA, MAAA,
and Oscar M. Lucas, ASA, MAAA

Traditional health care financial models do not readily lend themselves to the monitoring of reimbursement approaches that transfer risk to providers. Health care financial managers will find that actuarial cost models provide the right structures and data for such analyses. Financial managers can understand the risks facing their organizations only through understanding the variability of the models' actuarial assumptions. This chapter describes the basic concepts and uses of actuarial models as they apply to the measurement of health system risk.

Defining the Basic Elements of the Actuarial Cost Model

An *actuarial cost model* presents both the probability of an event occurring and the magnitude (cost) of that event. (In reality, both the probability and magnitude of events in health care reflect the variability of underlying processes.) For inpatient care, an actuarial cost model would include the following data for each type of patient (commercially insured, Medicare, and so on):

- *Admit rate:* This is the probability of a volume of admissions to a hospital during a period of time, usually expressed as an annual admit rate per 1,000 persons (admits/1,000). The 1,000 persons represents the underlying population base that generates the admitted patients.
- *Average length of stay (ALOS):* This identifies the duration of inpatient stays expressed in days.
- *Bed days:* This is the product of the admit rate and the ALOS, usually expressed as bed days per 1,000 persons per year.
- *Cost per day:* The cost per day could be based on gross charges, net

7

charges, average community charges, marginal cost, totally allocated cost, or fixed cost. It usually is projected to a specific time period to recognize the impact of inflation.

- *Per capita claims cost:* This is the product of the bed days and the cost per day divided by 1,000. It often is further divided by 12 to present a monthly cost. Managed care plans often refer to this as the per member per month (PMPM) cost.

The items in the model may reflect anticipated statistics (to forecast future results), historical data (for retrospective analysis), or current figures (for operational decisions). Analysis of actual to expected results (variance analysis) based on actuarial models can provide early warning signs of financial, operational, or clinical practice problems. The model can also establish anticipated utilization and costs to benchmark ongoing experience.

An actuarial cost model usually presents information for a large number of service categories, such as inpatient medical stays, surgical stays, obstetric stays, skilled nursing facility stays, and so on. More elaborate inpatient models may allocate costs by DRG categories. The level of detail depends on the operations to be examined; for example, subcapitation for organ transplants would normally require analyzing transplant DRGs. At a minimum, a model for a full-service system usually includes information on inpatient hospital, outpatient hospital, physician services by type of service, prescription drugs, and other categories. An illustrative model is shown in table 2-1.

The actuarial cost model provides useful information for provider contracting. From the managed care plan's perspective, the average cost per service or cost per day assumption can translate into acceptable per diem rates. The product of the LOS and the cost per day yields per case costs that the financial manager can use to determine acceptable case rates. Similarly, a financial manager can determine the per diem or per case rates that are actuarially equivalent to a proposed capitation rate. (See chapter 3 for a more complete discussion of these reimbursement approaches.)

Insurance carriers and managed care plans develop actuarial cost models to project health care costs and establish premium rates. An actuarial model often begins with national average data, but must be modified to reflect the relevant local statistics, plan design (such as patient cost sharing), and the demographics of the population served. Health care actuaries are trained in the skills required to develop and apply this type of information.

Making Difficult Assumptions: Admission Rates, Case Mix, and Efficiency

The actuarial cost model shown in table 2-1 uses the assumptions of 89 admits/1,000, 5.75 days LOS, and $1,800 cost per day—all key information for a hos-

Table 2-1. Example of an Actuarial Cost Model (Beneficiaries under Age 65, Unmanaged System)

Type of Service	Annual Admits per 1,000	Length of Stay	Annual Utilization per 1,000	Average Cost per Service	Per Member Monthly Claim Cost
Hospital					
Inpatient	89	5.75	510	$1,800	$76.50
Outpatient			700	310	18.08
Physician					
Surgeries			480	580	23.20
Office visits			2,600	50	10.83
Radiology			800	120	8.00
Pathology			2,100	40	7.00
Other			3,200	90	24.00
Other					
Prescription drugs			4,300	40	14.33
Miscellaneous other			220	250	4.58
Total			14,910		$186.52

Source: Milliman & Robertson, Inc.

pital under risk contracts. Can the hospital perform at the level of 89 admits/1,000 at the indicated level of costs in comparison to revenue? Hospitals track admissions but will experience difficulty in adequately determining their *rate* of admission. As shown in the section on assessing the degree of health care management later in this chapter, a higher-than-normal admit rate may indicate that more vigilant care management is needed.

Comparing unadjusted LOS can be biased since they do not reflect variations in case mix and acuity/severity mix. To illustrate, treating patients in the most cost-efficient setting can include shifting less severe cases to an outpatient or home health care setting. The remaining inpatient cases have a higher acuity. In theory (and sometimes in actuality), this can cause an effective high-quality delivery system to have a longer average inpatient LOS than an inefficient system. However, generally the most efficient health care managers can reduce LOS such that the aggregate average LOS is lower than in inefficient systems.

The providers and payers must understand both experience and assumptions in terms of case mix and results adjusted for acuity/severity. Both the admit rate and case mix affect the assessment of the cost per day. Often a higher-than-normal admit rate is associated with a higher-than-normal LOS, both having an impact on the cost per day. Because the cost per day is generally higher during the early days of a stay, the average cost per day tends to increase as the LOS decreases. As managed care systems focus on reducing unnecessary days and admits, there will be an impact on the assumptions for cost per day and on provider cost structures.

Developing Actuarial Cost Models

Actuarial cost models are only as good as the data and actuarial judgment used to make them. Following are *general* rules to keep in mind about health system cost models:

- Rapid changes in health care cost, managed care efficiency, and delivery systems underscore the need for the most recent data possible.
- A more substantial data base (in terms of size and scope) generally will produce more credible results. Utilization rates, in particular, can fluctuate from one time period to another. Inadequate data can lead to inappropriate assumptions, which potentially can lead to disappointing results.
- Data from traditional fee-for-service systems need adjustment for managed care systems. Information about type of service and unit charge or unit cost information can be useful. However, this information is inadequate in terms of the impact of managed care or changes in the degree of health care management.

Sources of data for developing actuarial cost models include:

- Actuarial consulting firms specializing in work with providers and carriers
- State insurance department rate filings made by HMOs or other health plans
- Hospital cost report filings (such as those for Medicare)
- State-administered data bases (including hospital discharge surveys)
- Publicly available Medicare and Medicaid information
- Health care industry surveys (such as those done by the Health Insurance Association of America [HIAA])
- Insurance company data

Additional resources listed at the end of this publication offer some useful points of contact. The following paragraphs describe some caveats about the sources listed above.

Actuarial consulting firms specializing in health care risk have meaningful data, but models based on these data should always be reconciled against other known information. A model's users should understand their environment, including significant differences from providers in other regions.

State insurance department rate filings of HMOs and insurance companies are generally available to the public. Sometimes, rate filings clearly document the assumptions used by HMOs and Blue Cross/Blue Shield plans and can thus provide useful figures to compare to a model's assumptions (and filings may also include data on financial performance and volume of business). Unfortunately, there are many ways that a company may categorize its health care costs; therefore, the analyst will need to carefully compare the figures in rate filings to those used in his or her model. In addition, states differ in their auditing of rate filings, with the result that information in rate filings could prove unreliable for comparative purposes.

An individual hospital's cost reports are useful to the extent that the hospital reported accurate data. However, if hospitals have submitted poor-quality data, different hospital reports can be hard to reconcile.

State-administered hospital discharge record data bases are excellent resources for developing meaningful benchmarks for both unmanaged and managed care assumptions. Because states often tabulate this information by DRG, the data can be used to analyze both variations in charges and distribution of stays and days by DRG. The more elaborate actuarial cost models present utilization and cost information by DRG.

Medicare and Medicaid information also can prove useful. In particular, Medicare's data files provide detailed physician information by CPT code. However, because the level and type of services provided to Medicare and Medicaid populations differ from those provided to commercial populations, these data have serious limitations for direct application to commercial situations. However, these files do provide useful geographic information regarding net charges by CPT code.

Health care industry surveys examine how costs vary by area and the relative costs of different procedures or categories of care. For example, the HIAA publishes information reported by its members that shows the distribution of physician charges by CPT-4 code and by three-digit zip code. This "prevailing fee" information from the fee-for-service environment can help health systems estimate the cost savings that a particular discounted fee schedule can produce.

Claims data repositories such as health insurer data can provide useful information if properly analyzed. Because most insurers track the population base that generates claims, an actuary can use insurer data to link health claims to the age, sex, family status, and employment status of the individuals generating a given type of claim. Equally important, insurer data bases have information about who *does not* produce claims. Thus, insurer data bases can help develop admit rates and costs per 1,000 population.

However, insurer data bases contain their own flaws, including the likelihood that the data do not reflect managed care operations. Furthermore, the data will reflect an insurer's particular products and approaches to operations, reimbursement, underwriting, and marketing, and would likely require adjustments for other applications. Finally, most insurers guard their information and often will not release the data base.

Assessing the Degree of Health Care Management

A system's ability to successfully assume and manage risk directly relates to its ability to successfully work with individual health care providers. The degree of health care management is an effective way of measuring the system's management ability.

Health care management focuses on the way health care services are delivered. The degree of health care management increases as a health system modifies behavior to be more efficient or offer increased quality. The degree of health care management could be compared to a flow meter. A 0 percent degree of health care management produces only "unmanaged" care (traditional fee-for-service levels of utilization and cost); a 100 percent degree of health care management produces optimal managed care. The degree of health care management helps define the underlying assumptions for actuarial cost models.

Figure 2-1 provides a visual illustration of the degree of health care management concept. The upper diagonal represents PMPM costs at undiscounted or community average reimbursement levels for delivery systems with degrees of health care management ranging from 0 percent (traditional fee-for-service levels of utilization and cost) to 100 percent (optimally managed). Similarly, the lower diagonal represents PMPM costs at discounted reimbursement levels with varying degrees of health care management. The PMPM cost for a system currently managing at 50 percent degree of health care management is indicated by point A. For the delivery system to meet a proposed target cost of $115 PMPM, indicated by the horizontal broken line, the degree of health care management must be increased to 90 percent as indicated by point B, or reimbursement levels discounted as indicated by point C. An appropriate mix of increased degree of health care management and increased discount would produce the same result.

An *optimal delivery system,* both actuarially and clinically, may be defined as one having ideal utilization levels in terms of efficiency and quality. Although the optimal system has the least medically unnecessary care, it still delivers some unnecessary care because medicine is not a perfect science. Providers may deliver some care that retrospectively may appear greater than needed; however, on a prospective basis the care was reasonable based on the information available to the provider at the time of service.

Two effective ways to gauge a system's degree of health care management are:

- An actuarial analysis of historical delivery system results
- A clinical review of patient charts

Generally, a system will assess its management capabilities by using both approaches.

Figure 2-1. Visual Representation of the Concept of Degree of Health Care Management

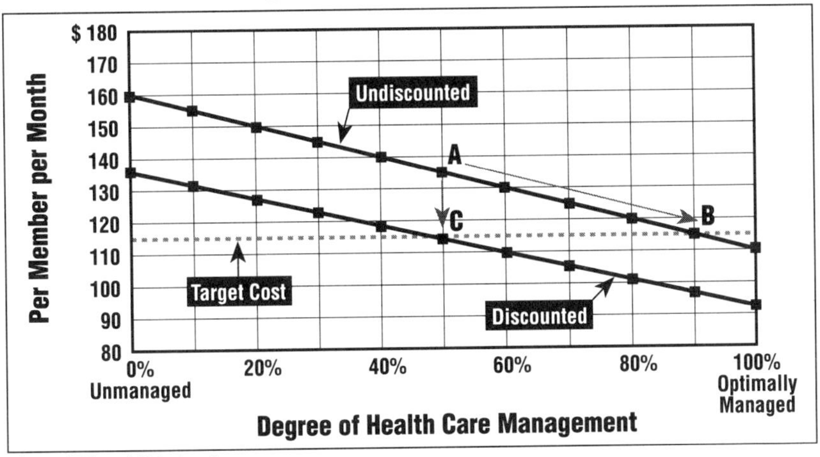

Source: Milliman & Robertson, Inc.

Actuarial Analysis

The actuarial analysis begins by gathering historical data, which can prove more challenging than it sounds. At a minimum, the analysis should include the following information (which is often available from UB-92 forms):

- Patient age and sex
- Assigned DRG
- LOS
- Type of payer (including commercial, HMO, PPO, Medicare, Medicaid)
- Gross charges
- Net charges

Additional helpful data include costs, transfer status (from or to another hospital), ICD-9 diagnostic and procedures codes, readmission information, and whether the patient died prior to discharge. With this information, the actuary can accurately compare system performance to standards or benchmarks.

Benchmarks should reflect specific underlying assumptions such as demographic mix, case mix, and acuity/severity mix. Given these assumptions, data on unmanaged care reflect the practice patterns of a specific geographic area. By contrast, the corresponding optimal benchmarks could apply to almost any geographic region. A basic calculation of the degree of health care management includes:

- Using the hospital's actual distribution of cases by DRG, recalculate composite LOS from both the unmanaged and optimally managed care standards by DRG.
- For each DRG, and also for the composites, interpolate the system's

position on the spectrum. If the LOS is lower than the optimal, assume 100 percent management. If the LOS is longer than the local fee-for-service average, assume 0 percent. For an LOS falling between the two endpoints, calculate its relative position on the spectrum. For example, if the traditional fee-for-service LOS is 5.00 and the optimal LOS is 3.00, a reported LOS of 4.50 would be calibrated as a 25 percent degree of health care management (25 percent of the way between 5.00 and 3.00).

• Separate calculations for commercial and Medicare patients, because these populations have very different utilization patterns.

The above process does not compensate for variations in demographic mix or severity/acuity mix. The recompositing of standard LOS using the hospital's actual case mix automatically adjusts for case-mix variances. The relationship between the standard composite and the case-mix–adjusted composite provides a numerical measure of case-mix bias that also can clarify the types of patients a hospital treats.

Unless a hospital treats all patients in a particular geographic area or only receives patients from a specific closed group, it is very difficult to develop realistic admit rates based on the hospital's own data. When a provider contract is exclusive for a closed group, the hospital can calculate its admit rate per 1,000 people. Health care systems (including HMOs and insurers) will use the admit rate as a key factor in evaluating delivery system performance.

Recognizing the problems with admit rates, the analysis described here produces an LOS degree of health care management. A better analysis of health care management effectiveness would be based on bed days, a product of LOS and admit rate. Using LOS or bed days, however, allows the actuary to establish utilization and cost assumptions for the model.

Some other useful analyses can be completed with these same data. These include the following:

• *Targeted improvement:* The DRG-specific degree of health care management calculations described above could be sorted by increasing degree of health care management for higher-volume or higher-cost procedures. This provides a shopping list of which DRGs would yield the greatest return if improved toward optimal.

• *Charge comparisons:* Historical charge information can be compared to case-mix–adjusted norms to show how competitive the charges are. With information on gross charges, net charges, and cost, a total comparison results.

• *Degree of health care management by line of business:* A financial or clinical manager can compare the degree of health care management for different types of patients to evaluate whether performance varies in efficiency for HMO patients over traditional indemnity insurance patients.

- *Service filtering:* Historical data analysis can isolate those services (DRG categories) delivered at and below threshold levels. If a service falls below a specified threshold frequency, managed care programs may require the hospital to refer that service to a different institution— even if the hospital receives a full capitation for all services. The hospital must set aside part of the capitation rate for care provided in a different facility.

The filtering process offers an indication of the care that the hospital can or should deliver internally, but it also quantifies the assumptions by DRG to provide both utilization and cost information. Hospital management can use this analysis of expected utilization and cost information to determine the feasibility of investing in programs to handle those DRGs that it would currently refer elsewhere.

Chart Review and Severity Adjustments

No actuarial analysis reflects individual patient acuity/severity. Acuity/severity adjustments require examination of individual patient charts. A qualified clinician (usually a physician) pulls a stratified random sample of inpatient charts for review. Through retrospective review and with reference to optimally efficient practice standards or practice guidelines, the clinician reviews the care provided to individual patients and tries to identify what care was appropriate, inappropriate, necessary, and unnecessary.

This process identifies the percentage of unnecessary admits, perfect stays (or those without unnecessary care), and unnecessary days. This usually requires a minimum sample size of 100 for statistical reliability. With appropriate stratification, the sample can balance the actuarial analysis to more precisely estimate the degree of health care management in that institution.

Grouping of results by admitting physician also can provide insight into which physicians might be good candidates for formation of an integrated delivery system (IDS). This analysis, however, requires a much larger sample of chart reviews.

Assuming a random sample that fairly represents the care provided at the studied facility, variations in the composite LOS by type of case indicates the types of patients that receive care and a crude measure of acuity/severity. Table 2-2 (p.16) presents this process.

The analysis in table 2-2 assumes that both a basic degree of health care management calculation and inpatient chart reviews have been completed for the hospital's commercial patients. Lines 1 and 2 summarize standardized assumptions for the unmanaged and optimal system, showing the admits/1,000, days/1,000, and ALOS. These assumptions have been tailored to the hospital's geographic area. Additionally, an average commercial population with average case mix and average severity has been assumed. These assumptions are shown excluding well newborn babies, consistent with standard HMO measures of

Table 2-2. Analysis of Bed Days Degree of Health Care Management and Case Mix/Severity, Commercial Population for Community Hospital

	Excluding Well Newborns			Including Well Newborns		
	Admits per 1,000	Days per 1,000	LOS	Cases per 1,000	Days per 1,000	LOS
Standard Assumptions						
1. Unmanaged utilization	72.3	320.0	4.43	84.1	348.3	4.14
2. Optimally managed utilization	57.4	179.6	3.13	69.6	200.2	2.88
Medical Chart Review Results						
3. Percent unnecessary	1%	13%				
4. Implied utilization (before case-mix/severity adjustment)	58.0	206.4	3.56			
5. Bed days degree of health care management (before case-mix/ severity adjustment)		81%				

Case-Mix and Severity Index	
6. Optimal LOS by DRG applied to hospital case mix	2.61
7. Estimated LOS case-mix index	0.91
8. Chart review—observed LOS	3.06
9. Chart review—necessary LOS	2.69
10. Necessary ratio	0.88
11. Actual LOS	2.82
12. Estimated necessary LOS	2.48
13. Estimated severity index	0.95
14. LOS case-mix/severity index	0.86

Formulas:

(4) Implied utilization = (2) optimal utilization / [100% - (3) percent unnecessary]
(5) Bed days degree of management = [(1) unmanaged days - (4) implied days] / [(1) unmanaged days - (2) optimal days]
(6) Calculated as the composite of each DRG's optimal target ALOS with the number of admissions in that DRG (calculation not shown)
(7) Estimated LOS case mix = (6) optimal LOS by DRG / (2) optimal LOS for all commercial members
(8) The ALOS of the audited patient charts (calculation not shown)
(9) The necessary ALOS of the audited patient charts (calculation not shown)
(10) Necessary ratio = (9) necessary LOS / (8) observed LOS
(11) The ALOS from the hospital's commercial population experience
(12) Estimated necessary ratio = (10) necessary ratio x (11) actual LOS
(13) Estimated severity index = (12) estimated necessary LOS / (6) optimal LOS adjusted for DRG case mix
(14) Estimated case-mix / severity index = (7) estimated LOS case mix x (13) estimated severity index

Source: Milliman & Robertson, Inc.

admissions and inpatient days. Then, the admits/1,000 and days/1,000 are shown including well newborn babies, consistent with standard hospital measures of utilization.

Lines 3 and 4 summarize results from the inpatient chart review process. The process suggests that 1 percent of the admits and 13 percent of the days in the period studied were medically unnecessary. These values can be applied to the optimally managed standards to project anticipated commercial utilization assumptions for the institution. Line 5 presents an overall degree of health care management for inpatient care prior to case-mix severity adjustments (calculated using the formula shown at the bottom of table 2-2). These utilization levels and degree of health care management assume that the chart review was a statistically reliable characterization of the hospital's case mix and severity.

Line 6 comes from a degree of health care management statistical calculation discussed earlier in this chapter and presents the optimal LOS based on the hospital's distribution of admissions by DRG. Comparing this LOS to the line 2 LOS determines the LOS case-mix index in line 7. Lines 8 and 9 come from a chart review process discussed earlier in this chapter and are used to determine a necessary ratio in line 10. The necessary ratio is the portion of the total LOS observed in the detailed chart review that was determined to be medically necessary. Again, a correctly designed statistical sample of chart review cases will help ensure that this factor fairly represents all commercial patients at the institution.

The necessary ratio is applied to the actual LOS to project an estimated necessary LOS, or what the LOS would have been if care had been optimal. The difference between this LOS and that shown in line 6 is the estimate of the severity difference. To the extent that this adjusted LOS is greater than line 6, patients probably have higher-than-normal severity. To the extent that it is less than line 6, patients probably have lower-than-normal severity. Line 14 combines the case-mix and severity indices for an overall value. This factor quantifies the overall difference between the optimal model LOS (line 2) and the estimated necessary LOS (line 12).

Based on table 2-2, the hospital has an overall LOS case-mix index of 91 percent and a severity index of 95 percent. Therefore, the case mix and severity experienced is 86 percent (91 percent x 95 percent) of the experience of the standard commercial population.

Thus, this process provides a more realistic estimate of the degree of health care management than either chart reviews or data analysis alone, although it still involves broad assumptions as to the consistency of severity between those charts reviewed and all cases.

Using Actuarial Models for Strategic Planning

An actuarial cost model can be used to project optimal bed supply and optimal member size to fill a hospital. Assuming an 85/15 percent weighting of commercial and Medicare patients, it can be estimated that the *current* national average inpatient utilization stands at about 750 bed.days/1,000 people. By comparison, our projected *optimal* utilization would be about 320 bed.days/

1,000 people. Assuming full capacity at 85 percent occupancy, a 500-bed facility has the potential to provide 155,125 days of care during a year (500 x 365 x .85). At *current* utilization levels, this suggests that it takes about 206,833 members to fill that hospital (155,125 x 1000/750), or a ratio of 2.42 beds/1,000 people. However, at *optimal* utilization levels, it would take 484,766 members to fill that hospital (155,125 x 1,000/320), a ratio of only about 1.03 beds/1,000.

Table 2-3 shows our estimates of excess capacity in several markets to illustrate the seriousness of the competitive risk in these markets in light of the projected optimal level of 1.03 beds/1,000 target. Currently, there are three to six beds per 1,000 people in most metropolitan markets. These calculations show the potential for increased competitive pressure (compared with today) as systems proceed toward optimal utilization patterns under managed care.

Producing Management Information for Health Systems

Successful management of the health care system and its related risk will require good management information. Historically, hospitals have had difficulty producing good cost information by type of service or type of patient. Cost accounting systems will need improvement as payers demand additional demonstrations of the effective management of patients. Key information for provider management of risk includes:

- Financial
    - Profit/loss by payer and contract type
    - Detailed allocation of expenses by product line
    - Calculations of incurred-but-not-reported (IBNR) expense—outstanding payments to other providers
    - Risk/incentive fund allocations
- Clinical
    - Unnecessary admits
    - Unnecessary days
    - Readmission rates
    - Mortality rates
    - Quality scores (such as Health Plan Employer Data and Information Set [HEDIS] score)
    - Automated patient records
    - Referral rates

Table 2-3. Estimated Excess Capacity in Selected Metropolitan Areas

Area	Beds per 1,000	% Excess Capacity
Atlanta	3.20	211%
Baltimore	3.47	237%
Birmingham	6.00	482%
Boston	2.56	149%
Chicago	3.25	216%
Cincinnati	3.83	272%
Cleveland	4.46	333%
Dallas–Ft. Worth	2.77	169%
Denver	3.21	212%
Des Moines	5.30	414%
Detroit	3.52	242%
Hartford	2.17	110%
Honolulu	2.51	144%
Houston	4.02	290%
Indianapolis	3.98	287%
Kansas City	4.42	329%
Las Vegas	2.28	121%
Little Rock	5.79	462%
Los Angeles	3.16	207%
Louisville	3.44	234%
Memphis	5.02	388%
Miami	4.61	348%
Milwaukee	3.55	245%
Minneapolis–St. Paul	2.95	186%
New Orleans	4.96	382%
New York–Newark	3.74	263%
Norfolk	2.81	173%
Oklahoma City	4.28	315%
Philadelphia	4.22	309%
Phoenix	2.75	167%
Pittsburgh	4.51	338%
Portland	2.66	158%
Salt Lake City	2.67	159%
San Diego	2.50	143%
San Francisco	2.71	163%
Seattle	2.34	127%
St. Louis	4.88	374%
Tampa	4.01	289%
Washington, DC	2.55	147%
Nationwide	3.73	262%

Sources: *AHA Hospital Statistics*. Chicago, IL: American Hospital Association, 1992; and Statistical Abstract of the United States, 1993.

- Actuarial
  - — Degree of health care management by type of service/patient
  - — Case-mix–adjusted LOS
  - — Adjusted per diem and per case rates by patient type/payer
  - — Comparisons to community norms
  - — Variance analysis

How Do Providers Assume and Control Risk?

Timothy D. Lee, FSA, MAAA

HMOs, PPOs, insurance carriers, and employers shift risk to the providers of health care through contractual reimbursement arrangements. For the past several decades, carriers paid health care providers fee-for-service payments based on the provider's billed charges, with only a usual, customary, and reasonableness test or discounts applied to the level of billed charges. With no real control over the level of charges or the utilization of health care services, the carriers retained the entire risk that health care costs for their insured population would be different from the risk they anticipated when they set their premium rates. This chapter examines the nature of risk underlying the different approaches to reimbursement and the tools providers use to control these risks.

Risk Shifting in Reimbursement Approaches

Managed care contracts now have provisions that shift risk to providers through guaranteed discounts off billed charges, per diem rates, per case rates, and capitation payments.

Guaranteed Discounts off Billed Charges

Discounts achieve lower costs for carriers but have only a minor impact on the risk to providers. The provider's risk is that price will not cover costs given the difficulty in projecting revenues when part of the provider's patient base will be paying at a level of charges lower than the rest of the patient base. This risk is akin to the difficulty for the provider in projecting the level of bad debt expense and other nonpayment.

Per Diem Rates

Under per diem contracts, hospital reimbursement is a previously agreed-on dollar amount for each patient bed day. These contracts often cover facility charges only, but sometimes also cover hospital-based physicians. This fixed-payment approach shifts from the insurance carrier to the provider the risk that actual costs per day will be more or less than expected. A single per diem covering all hospital stays shifts the most risk to the hospital, because the hospital is at risk that the patient case mix will differ from prior experience or from demographic and epidemiological studies that support the per diem. Per diem arrangements by service or DRG shifts much less risk to the hospital, because increased service intensity is reimbursed at higher payment levels.

Per Case Rates

Medicare uses a per case approach to reimbursing hospitals, making a single payment based on the diagnosis. This approach not only shifts the risk to the hospital that the level of charges (that is, the intensity of care provided) will be greater than expected, but also shifts the risk that the length of stay (LOS) will be longer than expected. Unlike the per diem approach that pays more money for a long LOS, the case rate approach yields the same amount of money for a long LOS as for a short LOS.

As with the per diem approach, a single case rate for all types of admissions transfers the case-mix risk to the providers. Case rates that vary by every DRG essentially keep the case-mix risk with the insurance carrier. The risk that the frequency of hospital admissions will be more or less than expected also stays with the insurance carrier under case rate approaches.

As inpatient utilization has declined, many hospitals are providing more outpatient services. In response to increased hospital-based outpatient utilization and charges, managed care organizations have more aggressively contracted on a fixed rate per case for outpatient services. These types of arrangements are most common on outpatient surgery facility charges and emergency department (ED) services. Some contracts vary the case rates by type of surgery or type of ED use, which allows for a better match of revenue to the hospital's cost of delivering the service. Such varying outpatient case rates shift less risk to the hospital than would a flat case rate that applies to all surgeries or all ED visits.

Capitation Payments

Capitation payments, which are based on a per member per month (PMPM) fee for each enrollee in the plan, shifts from insurance carriers to the hospitals the risk that:

- The frequency of admits will be more than expected.

- The level of charges or intensity of services provided will be more than expected.
- The case mix will be more severe than expected.

Under a capitation contract, the hospital essentially underwrites the risk for the scope of services that fall under its contract with the carrier.

Table 3-1 summarizes which organization, the managed care organization or the hospital, has the risk of adverse experience in each of the various risk categories.

Risk Shifting through Risk Pools and Withholds

Whichever reimbursement method is chosen, there are ways in which the managed care organization, physicians, and the hospital can share in the financial risk for hospital services. (It is common for physicians to share in the financial risk for hospital services because they generally have more influence over the use of hospital services than do hospitals.) The use of risk pools and withholds can accomplish this risk sharing.

The traditional approach to a hospital risk pool is to establish a budget on a PMPM basis for hospital services. The budget, or expected cost, would be set for a fixed period of time, usually 12 months. The total budgeted dollars would be the budgeted amount PMPM times the number of members enrolled for each month.

Table 3-1. Who Has the Risk of Adverse Experience?

Reimbursement Approach	Type of Risk			
	Level of Charge (Intensity of Services) Risk	LOS Risk	Number of Admits Risk	Case-Mix Risk
Discounted fee-for-service	M	M	M	M
Single per diem	H	M	M	H
Per diems varying by DRG	H	M	M	M
Single case rate	H	H	M	H
Case rates varying by DRG	H	H	M	M
Capitation	H	H	H	H

Note: H = hospital
M = managed care organization

At the end of the contract period, the total actual expenses would be compared to budgeted amounts. Although enough time should be allowed after the end of the contractual period so that most claims have been paid, it is common for an allowance to be added to the expenses for the expected outstanding claims.

If the actual expenses are less than the budgeted expenses, there would be "surplus" that would be distributed to the various parties. If the actual amount exceeds the budgeted amount, the deficit would be shared among the appropriate parties. Typically, the deficit recovery would occur in one of two ways:

- *Provider payment withhold:* The insurance carrier retains a portion of the amount that otherwise would have been paid to the provider. For example, a 10 percent withhold would mean that 90 percent of the agreed-on amount would be paid to the hospital or physician at the time the claim was adjudicated. The remaining 10 percent would be "withheld" and returned at the end of the contract period if there were a surplus. If there were a deficit, the withhold would be used to cover all or part of the deficit. Withholds are used most commonly with physician risk pools because administering cash settlements from large numbers of physicians is difficult.
- *End-of-year cash settlement:* The hospital is required to pay the managed care organization an amount equal to its share of the deficit or the amount would be withheld from future payments to the hospital.

An example of a hospital risk pool surplus allocation is shown in table 3-2 (p.25).

Risk Shifting with Multiple-Year Contracts

Multiple-year contracts with managed care organizations bring additional financial risks, also certain advantages. The obvious financial risk is that neither the managed care organization nor the hospital knows the rate of future cost increases. Thus, if costs increase more rapidly than expected, the escalator built into the contract may be too low. A related risk occurs when the initial capitation rate is too low, as when the assumed utilization rate per 1,000 is significantly less than can be achieved. In this case, the hospital will have to continue being significantly underreimbursed for the length of the contract.

The advantage to a hospital of a multiple-year contract is the ability to budget and plan for a longer time period. The hospital is protected against decreases in capitation or significantly lower increases than expected. In addition, the hospital may feel more secure about its revenue stream from the managed care organization.

Table 3-2. Example of Risk Pool Surplus Allocation

Budgeted amount	$30.00 PMPM
Actual contractual amount	$28.00 PMPM
Surplus	$ 2.00 PMPM
Allocation of surplus	
Managed care organization	40% = $0.80 PMPM
Physicians	30% = $0.60 PMPM
Hospital	30% = $0.60 PMPM

Tools That Providers Can Use to Control Risk

The tools to manage risk under a reimbursement contract with a managed care organization fall into three general categories. These are:

- *Contractual tools:* These relate to modifications that would be made in the reimbursement contract to control or limit the extent to which risk is transferred.
- *Health care delivery management tools:* These relate to the methods that the provider uses in carrying out its main line of business, which is the actual delivery of health care services.
- *Business tools:* These relate to general management techniques that can be used to manage any type of business risk.

Contractual Tools

The following sections describe approaches to contractual protections against adverse experience.

Stop-Loss Insurance

A common contract provision is for additional payments to be made by the carrier to the hospital on catastrophic claims. For example, a *catastrophic claim* might be defined as one in which the hospital's billed charges exceed $50,000 on an individual patient. The $50,000 threshold operates as a deductible. When the threshold is exceeded, the stop-loss insurance carrier would assume liability for, perhaps, 90 percent of all charges in excess of $50,000. The hospital might obtain this stop-loss insurance through its contract with the managed care organization, or it could purchase it from a company specializing in such insurance.

Outlier Payments

Outlier payments would be made by the managed care organization on cases in which the contractual reimbursement to the hospital varied significantly from the billed charges incurred by the patient. Theoretically, the outlier provisions of a contract could either increase the reimbursement to a hospital or decrease it on a particular case

For example, an outlier provision under a case rate reimbursement approach might say that whenever the case rate is less than 50 percent of actual billed charges, the managed care organization will make a supplemental payment to the hospital to bring the total reimbursement for that case up to the level of 50 percent of billed charges. It also may say that whenever the case rate reimbursement is greater than 80 percent of billed charges on a particular patient, the case rate will be reduced for that patient so that the hospital does not receive more than 80 percent of billed charges in total reimbursement.

Risk-Sharing Provisions

There are contractual provisions that can allow the hospital and the managed care organization to share the risk of adverse claims experience. Methods for sharing this risk could include a combination of:

- *An experience refund provision:* In this method, if capitation payments exceed actual billed charges by some predetermined amount, the excess amounts (or some percentage thereof) will be refunded to the managed care organization.
- *A supplemental capitation provision:* In this method, if the actual billed charges exceed the capitation payments by some predetermined amount over the course of the year for the entire enrollment group, the managed care organization will supplement its reimbursement to the hospital with additional capitation payments.

Both these techniques are common provisions in insurance carrier contracts with large self-funded employers and are becoming more common in provider reimbursement contracts.

Risk-Adjusted Capitation Rates

The capitation payments made by the managed care organization can be adjusted to reflect key indicators of the future health costs of the individual enrollees. The most common key indicators (risk characteristics) are the enrollee's age and sex, but certain health status indicators such as smoking also might be used. This type of risk classification for determining premium rates is a long-standing practice of insurance carriers. Indicators of health costs should be easily determinable, the cost differences should be measurable and material, and the indicators should be practical to implement.

Subcapitation to Other Providers

The hospital, which is the primary acceptor of the capitation rate and responsible for providing all contractual services, may choose to carve out some of those services and capitate them to a second provider under a separate contract. For example, a skilled nursing facility or a home health care agency might represent a good subcapitation prospect if the hospital does not provide these services. The hospital has thus limited its risk for the costs of providing these services by passing it on to another organization. Certain tertiary care services such as transplantations or burn treatments can also be subcapitated to other hospitals. The goal for the hospital would be to retain the risk only on those services over which it has some control.

Escalator Clauses in Multiple-Year Contracts

Multiple-year contracts commonly have an escalator clause that increases the rate of reimbursement for each 12-month period. This approach is superior to having a flat rate for the entire time period. The most common inflation escalator clauses are based on the consumer price index (CPI), using the all-items CPI or the medical care CPI. In each case, it is likely that the CPI understates the increase in hospital costs. As an alternative to using the national CPI, the escalator could be based on the CPI for the metropolitan area in which the hospital is located or for the nearest metropolitan area for which the CPI is calculated. Another alternative would be simply to have a fixed-percentage increase included in the contract (for example, 5 percent per year).

Health Care Delivery System Management Tools

Delivery system management tools include any methods or approaches leading to the more efficient delivery of health care services. Meeting or beating the targets implied in the reimbursement contract with respect to LOS, intensity of services provided, number of admissions, and so on depends on greater efficiency. The hospital needs to develop medical management strategies and work with its physicians to develop clinical guidelines, protocols, and treatment paths. Other activities might include:

- Recruitment and training of medical directors experienced in managed care
- Recruitment and training of nurses with managed care experience
- Development of utilization management guidelines for clinical care
- Development of case management guidelines

Analysis of the utilization of services will be a key component in measuring and modifying the efficiency of delivering health care services. For example, comparing actual experience with clinically developed target LOS by DRG is an effective approximation of the current level of health care management. Medical chart audits that examine the level of efficiency and severity of cases at the hospital also help improve the efficiency of health care delivery.

Resource planning is yet another tool to be used to help achieve the necessary levels of efficiency. Examination of historical utilization experience for closed population groups supports reasonable estimates about the resources needed as the capitated population grows. Resources such as the number of ICU beds, regular beds, MRI machines, operating rooms, hospital-based pathologists, and so on are dependent on the level of health care management existing in the system and on the risk characteristics of the population base (such as age and sex). Resource planning supports efficient use of resources and discourages overutilization of services for which the hospital is at risk.

General Business Tools for Managing Risk

Beyond seeking contractual protections and building systems to ensure optimal efficiency in health care delivery, health care executives should formulate a systematic approach to reviewing the operating assumptions of their managed care business. The following sections detail the key elements that should be a part of this ongoing review.

Risk Selection and Underwriting

The hospital will want to take all necessary steps, whether contractual, through observation, or through periodic auditing, to make sure the insurance carrier is following sound risk selection and underwriting guidelines.

Risk selection and underwriting (to the extent allowed by state insurance departments) is important in any insurance product line. As a hospital accepts risk transfer, it must evaluate the methods of risk selection and underwriting employed by the managed care organization. The hospital reimbursement rates in the contract are based on certain assumptions as to the health status of the insured population. It is important that the risk selection and underwriting techniques employed by the managed care organization be consistent with those that are assumed in the pricing of the insurance product and in the reimbursement rates for the hospital and other providers.

Market Assessment

Many "markets" may supply patients to providers, and each one has its own expected health care costs. Each of these markets also may require different levels of needed resources and different approaches to utilization management. Typical health insurance markets include:

- Large employer groups (typically with self-funded health benefit plans)
- Midsize employer groups (typically insured with insurance companies, Blue Cross/Blue Shield plans, or HMOs)
- Small employer groups (of fewer than 15 employees who make insurance purchasing decisions based primarily on price and, perhaps, on the specific health care needs of individual employees)
- Individuals (who purchase their own health insurance based on perceived need)
- Medicare (mostly the elderly, who, because of their age, have a variety of health care needs and often purchase insurance to fill the gaps in their Medicare coverage)
- Medicaid (the low-income population, who often have more health problems than the employee-related population and no family physician)

Each of these markets should be evaluated separately to capture the different cost expectations. For purposes of rating, projecting financial results, and analyzing financial experience, each market should be treated as a separate line of business. The analysis of financial results and the decisions about adjusting rates should be done for each market independent of the others.

Management Reporting

Good management reporting should be thorough, timely, and accurate. Management reports should give management the information to test all the assumptions that have been made in the product pricing. Management should track assumptions made in pricing with respect to utilization of services and the "average" charge per service. These assumptions should be tested by type of service (inpatient medical days, inpatient surgical days, outpatient surgeries, ED services, primary care services, specialist physician services, pathology, radiology, and so on). They also should be tested separately for each market or line of business.

For per diem contracts, management reports should match each service reimbursement category. For example, the contract may have a per diem for medical DRGs, surgical DRGs, ICU, and so on. For each service category, the hospital should track admits/1,000, ALOS, cost per day, allocated cost per day, and revenue per day. The contractual per diems should also be compared with the average charge per day and average cost per day to see if the underlying discount is reasonable or if the contract needs renegotiating.

Under a capitation contract, the hospital should capture encounter data and the associated billed charges. The hospital would compare the actual billed

charges and allocated costs for all services provided under the capitation contract to the capitation rate, plus any copayments received, plus coordination of
benefits and subrogation revenue, plus any incentive risk pool payments. This
comparison will reveal the effective discount in the capitation rate.

Additional management reporting should include tracking the hospital's
liability for any incentive pool payments to be made to the physicians or the
managed care organization. Additionally, the reporting should include claims
incurred but not reported for services performed by other providers for which
the hospital is liable (such as specialty hospitals to whom patients have been
referred by the hospital).

Financial Projections

Financial projections of revenues and expenses should be developed as part of
any feasibility study for a new venture. These projections can then be used as a
test against the realities of the marketplace to see if the new venture and products are feasible. Additionally, the projection acts as a budget once the new
venture is operational. A two-year financial projection probably is adequate in
the health care insurance market (although regulatory agencies may require
longer projections); projections beyond 24 months are less reliable due to changes
in health cost trends. Projections should be detailed by type of service, including specific budgeted line items for hospital inpatient services, outpatient surgery, emergency department, and so on, and should be updated frequently (perhaps quarterly, but at least semiannually) using actual data from experience
monitoring reports. A financial projection for hospital inpatient services for the
Medicare line of business might be formatted as shown in figure 3-1.

Monitoring Reports

Frequent monitoring of actual experience is essential if hospital management is
to make timely and informed repricing decisions. Experience monitoring warns
of revenue shortfalls and any needs to revise rates. A monitoring report might
take the format of figure 3-2. The hospital also needs to monitor the trends in
utilization and in PMPM cost to anticipate needed capitation revisions.

Periodic Price Adjustments

Monitoring experience and comparing it to budgeted costs allows adjustment
of prices with managed care organizations. For example, if the hospital's effective LOS declines, it can attempt to increase its market share by agreeing to

Figure 3-1. Sample Quarterly Financial Projection Report Format

	Months								
	January			February			March		
Medicare Risk Group	Total $	# of Days	Days per 1,000	Total $	# of Days	Days per 1,000	Total $	# of Days	Days per 1,000
Inpatient Hospital									
Medical									
Surgical									
ICU									
Maternity									
Psychiatric									

Figure 3-2. Sample Experience-Monitoring Report Format

	January					
	Days/Services per 1,000		Dollars of Expense		Charge per Day/Service	
	Budgeted	Actual	Budgeted	Actual	Budgeted	Actual
Hospital						
Medical						
Surgical						
ICU						
Maternity						
Psychiatric						
Physicians						
Primary care visits						
Specialty visits						
Inpatient surgeries						
Outpatient surgeries						

lower per case rates. However, a shorter LOS may mean that the hospital will need to increase its per diem rates under its per diem contracts to recognize the more intensive services provided on a daily basis for the shorter LOS. If the hospital's operating costs increase, a price increase in its per diem and case rates will be necessary to maintain its margins.

The hospital should monitor the market to see what price adjustments the market will allow and to charge accordingly. There is a tradition in health insurance of annual price adjustments to keep pace with inflation and other trends and to correct for past underestimates of health care costs. Managed care organizations and employers will anticipate that their providers will request annual price adjustments under their contracts.

Cost Structure

It is fundamental to successful financial management to know what it costs to bring a product or deliver a service to the market. A hospital should know its fixed and variable costs for delivering services under its contracts with managed care organizations. These costs are important to recognize for their impact on case rates if patient lengths of stay drop. Hospitals need to know how much costs have really been reduced by having a shorter LOS and, therefore, how much savings can be passed on to the managed care organization through a lower case rate. Many hospitals do not have adequate cost accounting systems, which means, among other things, that there is no cost history on which to base their pricing decisions. Until that cost history can be built up, the hospital will have to estimate its costs when developing its prices under its managed care contracts.

Chapter 4

What Is an Acceptable Contract?—A Capitation Case Study

Greg N. Herrle, FSA, MAAA, and David G. Ogden, FSA, MAAA

This chapter uses a simplified case study to illustrate some of the issues involved in assessing a capitation contract. A full assessment includes an analysis of the hospital's experience and capabilities, the organization offering the contract, and the competitive situation, as well as the details of the contract. Our case study assumes that the hospital has determined that it needs and wants the business available from the contract. In practice, a hospital's preliminary analysis should include an examination of whether it wants to do business with a particular managed care organization.

The Contract Proposal

Quality Health Plan (QHP), an HMO with 40,000 members, has proposed a contract to Neighborhood Hospital that would capitate the hospital for all inpatient hospital facility services on QHP's commercial group members whose primary care physician is affiliated with Neighborhood. QHP proposes to capitate Neighborhood at 35 percent of QHP's revenue with a minimum capitation of $30 per member per month (PMPM) for the upcoming contract year.

Evaluating the Adequacy of Capitation Rates

A key tool for evaluating the adequacy of QHP's capitation rates is the actuarial cost model. (See chapter 2.) The cost model includes utilization, average costs, and PMPM targets for a specified set of capitated services. The hospital can use information from the model to evaluate and prepare capitation proposals and to manage its business once a contract is signed.

The utilization, average costs, and PMPM targets in the actuarial cost model are unique to each contracting situation and are based on a number of key assumptions. These are:

- Contract period
- Geographical area
- Enrollment class (commercial group, Medicare, Medicaid)
- Local managed care utilization levels
- Level of health care management (from unmanaged to optimum, as defined in chapter 2)
- Patient cost sharing
- Target reimbursement levels
- Definition of capitated services
- Capitated services referred outside the hospital
- Historical experience costs of payer
- Historical managed care experience the hospital
- Payer's PMPM revenue (needed if the capitation contract is on a percentage of premium basis)
- Demographic mix of membership (for example, age and gender)

These assumptions are unique to each hospital and each contracting opportunity. Also, a given contract may include several distinct populations or benefits that should be analyzed separately. Clearly, capitation rates appropriate for one situation may not be appropriate for another.

The actuarial cost models in tables 4-1 and 4-2 (p. 36), which represent two different levels of health care management, have been developed to help Neighborhood Hospital evaluate the capitation proposal made by QHP. The utilization targets (expressed as days per 1,000 enrollees) under the loosely managed delivery system (table 4-1) represent a delivery system with limited health care management capabilities in Neighborhood's geographical area. The optimally managed utilization targets (table 4-2) represent "best observed practices" throughout the United States and illustrate the improvement potential under an optimally managed delivery system. The average costs per day are based on Neighborhood Hospital's target reimbursement, which equals 80 percent of its billed charges. The PMPM figure is a product of days per 1,000 and average cost per day divided by 1,000 and then further divided by 12.

The targets should be based on QHP's demographic mix. In fact, if the data are available, a cost model could be constructed based on QHP's historical experience.

Administrative costs and risk margins are added to the medical cost targets. Administrative costs will vary depending on the services included under the capitation agreement but could cover claims administration, utilization management, quality assurance, and member service functions. However, it should

Table 4-1. Actuarial Cost Model/QHP Capitation Analysis/In-patient Hospital Services—Loosely Managed Delivery System

Category of Service	Days per 1,000	Average Cost per Day	Per Member per Month
Medical	157	$1,500	$19.62
Surgical	132	1,800	19.80
Psychiatric	71	700	4.14
Alcohol and drug abuse	38	500	1.58
Maternity	42	1,500	5.25
Total medical costs	· 440	$1,374	$50.39
Administrative cost			$ 2.80
Risk margin			$ 2.80
Total			$55.99

Source: Milliman & Robertson, Inc.

be noted that although the hospital will incur administrative costs under a capitation contract, it often is difficult to get the payer to acknowledge the value of the administrative services performed by the hospital.

The medical cost targets in the actuarial cost model generally are established at best-estimate levels, which imply that the actual experience will be higher than the targets 50 percent of the time and lower than the targets 50 percent of the time. A risk margin should be added to the best-estimate medical cost targets to increase the probability that the capitation will exceed actual costs.

The QHP capitation proposal can now be evaluated by comparing the proposed capitation to the loosely managed and optimally managed targets of $55.99 and $26.95 PMPM, respectively. QHP's reported revenue equals $100 PMPM; thus, the estimated capitation equals $35 PMPM (35 percent of $100), with a minimum capitation of $30 PMPM.

Neighborhood can evaluate both the expected capitation and the minimum capitation against the targets in tables 4-1 and 4-2. A comparison of the tables is shown in table 4-3 (p. 37).

The expected QHP capitation of $35 PMPM is equal to 63 percent of the loosely managed target. With minimal health care management, the capitation would equate to only 63 percent of Neighborhood's fee targets or 50 percent of billed charges (63 percent x 80 percent). However, if Neighborhood could become optimally efficient, the QHP capitation would yield 130 percent of its target or 104 percent of billed charges (130 percent x 80 percent). This analysis also indicates that Neighborhood would have to perform about 37 percent ($35.00/$55.99 = 63 percent) better than a local unmanaged system to achieve

Table 4-2. Actuarial Cost Model/QHP Capitation Analysis/ Inpatient Hospital Services—Optimally Managed Delivery System

Category of Service	Days per 1,000	Average Cost per Day	Per Member per Month
Medical	79	$1,600	$10.53
Surgical	58	1,900	9.18
Psychiatric	13	800	0.87
Alcohol and drug abuse	4	600	0.20
Maternity	26	1,600	3.47
Total medical costs	180	$1,617	$24.25
Administrative cost			$ 1.35
Risk margin			$ 1.35
Total			$26.95

Source: Milliman & Robertson, Inc.

its fee targets (that is, achieve approximately 280 days per 1,000 rather than the 440 days calculated for a loosely managed system).

The actuarial cost models also can provide standards against which to compare actual experience after the capitated contract is signed. Variances in actual experience from the targets can be used to identify areas where improvements in efficiency or opportunities for savings could occur. More detailed versions of the actuarial cost model can further identify problem areas or opportunities. For example, the inpatient actuarial cost model could include targets by DRG or larger diagnostic groupings.

Neighborhood Hospital will need to address a number of issues in addition to the above development of actuarial cost models and capitation adequacy, including:

- The hospital's ability to educate and work with its physician staff to efficiently manage the use of inpatient health care services.
- The presence or creation of a physician incentive program to support its management objectives. In particular, can Neighborhood develop incentives for the physicians that will produce appropriate lengths of stay?
- The cost and risk of covering services provided at other hospitals (for example, tertiary services not available at Neighborhood Hospital). These services could be negotiated out of the capitation contract. However, if Neighborhood assumes the risk of these referral services, the actuarial cost model should be

Table 4-3. QHP Capitation Analysis

Proposed Capitation as Percentage of Targets		
Target	Estimated Capitation ($35 PMPM)	Minimum Capitation ($30 PMPM)
Loosely managed ($55.99 PMPM)	63%	54%
Optimally managed ($26.95 PMPM)	130%	111%

expanded to include utilization and cost targets for these services.

- Payers often will provide the hospital with some sort of stop-loss protection against large claims under a capitation contract. The payer
charges the hospital for this stop-loss coverage, usually by reducing
the capitation by a certain amount. This stop-loss charge should be
evaluated for reasonableness by obtaining an actuarial review or by
comparing the changes offered by the payer to the cost of purchasing
stop-loss coverage from an insurance carrier.
- The minimum capitation of $30 PMPM could be structured to vary by
member age and gender to better protect Neighborhood against the
risk of changes in QHP's membership.

Evaluating a Partner

Financial issues are not the only important considerations in evaluating the QHP
contract. These considerations should be reviewed in relationship to
Neighborhood's operational, financial, and marketing objectives. At this point,
it should be noted that the evaluation of any given partner should be made
against the background of the total marketplace. For example, the market in
Neighborhood Hospital's service area is extremely fragmented; no one payer
represents a significant portion of Neighborhood's revenue. Therefore, in the
short term, no one payer may be large enough to provide sufficient revenue to
Neighborhood, and Neighborhood will need to evaluate and contract with nu-
merous payers in the marketplace.

Market Share/Potential Volume

The QHP contract should be evaluated with respect to QHP's potential to bring
in new business to the hospital and to preserve Neighborhood's existing busi-

ness. QHP's historical growth rates and potential for new business in Neighborhood's service area should be assessed.

Product Diversity

Employer needs in Neighborhood's market are diverse, and many want the flexibility to choose from a multitude of products. Thus, QHP should be evaluated with respect to the array of products (HMOs, point-of-service plans, PPOs, and so on) it can offer successfully in the marketplace.

Contracting Strategy

QHP's delivery system philosophy can have a significant impact on Neighborhood's long-term financial success. For example, some delivery system structures are more favorable to hospitals than others. Some managed care systems place primary care physicians or groups at risk for the total health care dollar, and these primary care groups then contract on a fee-for-service basis with specialists and hospitals. Commodity pricing of hospital and specialty services may result, especially in markets with an oversupply of hospitals and specialists. Thus, in these situations, the hospital may find itself competing for business on a low-price basis, with little opportunity to share in a greater percentage of the health care dollar.

A more favorable structure would allow Neighborhood to share in a greater percentage of the health care dollar and also be more involved in the allocation and use of health care resources. An integrated approach that combines hospital and physician services with risk sharing and cooperative financial incentives for hospital and physician may place Neighborhood in a better position in the long run.

Systems and Administrative Support

Neighborhood should review QHP's management information systems prior to contracting with QHP. QHP's reporting capabilities should adequately support proper utilization management, physician profiling, and quality assurance programs.

Underwriting Capability

QHP's ability to adequately underwrite and price its products is important, because Neighborhood is at risk for hospital services. The hospital should review QHP's underwriting and pricing systems and continue to monitor these activities after the contract is implemented. In particular, if the capitation rate is set as a percent of the premium rate, Neighborhood should feel comfortable that premium rates are adequate and not extremely low to "buy" business.

Keys to Success under Capitation Contracts

Capitation represents a significant change from traditional fee-for-service reimbursement and will become a much more prevalent form of contracting in the future. Following are some of the keys to Neighborhood Hospital's success under the QHP capitation contract.

New Vision and Mind-set

Capitation contracting will require change in strategic vision and operations for Neighborhood Hospital. The strategy will make the transition from filling beds to managing the health care needs of a fixed population. All departments of the hospital will now become cost centers. One of the keys to Neighborhood's success will be to share a common vision and incentives with its physicians. (Table 4-4, outlines the key differences in approaches for capitation and fee-for-service contracts.)

Physician Incentive Program and Buy-in

Physicians control the use of hospital services, and they must be appropriately incented and involved in planning for success under capitation. The physicians and the hospital should have the same incentive to manage the use of health care resources appropriately. One approach is for Neighborhood to invest in physician education programs. Some portion of existing physician education programs, which Neighborhood already offers for obtaining continuing medical education credits, could be refocused on medical efficiency and the appropriate use of health care resources.

Medical Management

Another key to Neighborhood's success is the need to develop guidelines for the appropriate use of health care resources. Physicians must participate in, and buy in to, this guideline-setting process. Existing approaches referenced in the additional resources section of this publication can serve as a basis for the hospital's own standards.

Cost Accounting and Other Reporting Systems

Neighborhood will need a good cost accounting system to fully identify how and when costs and resources are used. It should be noted that the system must account for lines of business and buyer groups as well as traditional hospital accounting items.

Managed care information systems will be needed to measure costs, support

Table 4-4. Comparison of Core Concepts of Fee-for-Service and Capitated Systems

Fee for Service	Capitation
Revenue center	Cost center
Piecework	Fixed income
Maximize utilization	Manage utilization
Individual	Team
Payer concern: overutilization	Payer concern: underutilization
Small provider groups	Large, integrated groups
Primary care— less influence, less relative income	Primary care— more influence, more relative income
Past	Future

management of care, and evaluate required health care outcomes. These systems will need to support measurement of actual costs against the targets in the actuarial cost model for each contract. In addition, the hospital should have a physician profiling system that supports analysis of physician performance related to hospital-based care, both for individuals and for groups of physicians.

Administrative Services

Under the QHP capitated contract, it will be important to identify who is responsible for what services. The hospital will need to negotiate with QHP for part of QHP's administrative fee. However, this may be difficult because QHP is not likely to give the hospital much credit for its administrative service contribution.

Need for Subcontractors

Neighborhood Hospital may be capitated for a wide range of services, including inpatient, outpatient, home health, ambulance, and so on. However, the hospital may need to subcontract for services it cannot or does not provide, including certain tertiary services. In these situations, Neighborhood will need to contract with other providers to offer such services. The hospital may utilize QHP's existing reimbursement rates with these providers or negotiate a new reimbursement arrangement. The relationship with subcontracted providers also has a risk and should be as carefully evaluated as that with a managed care organization.

Evaluating Performance/Renewal Contracting

Neighborhood Hospital should plan how it will gather information needed to evaluate the success of the capitation contract with QHP and, ultimately, to decide whether to renew.

Cost Structure and Income Allocation

Neighborhood will need to identify and correctly allocate its costs associated with QHP patients to evaluate the ongoing financial success of the QHP contract. Similarly, Neighborhood will need to know what income it has earned from the QHP contract, including capitation payments and patient copays. With this information, decisions can be made about renewal or renegotiation of rates.

Comparison to Expectations

A comparison of Neighborhood's actual utilization and costs to the actuarial cost model targets (as illustrated in tables 4-1 and 4-2) should be made on a routine basis. This comparison will help identify problem areas and potential solutions. It also will help support business decisions with respect to negotiating the renewal of the QHP contract.

Performance of Partner

Neighborhood Hospital should evaluate its relationship with QHP and whether QHP is performing at the level required under the contract prior to renewal. This evaluation could include issues such as enrollment levels, data reporting, presence of competing providers, timeliness of payments, and other matters. Additionally, the quality of the relationship and services of QHP should be assessed. Provider–managed care relationships are sometimes too burdensome or contentious to be worth maintaining.

What Strategies Will Promote Physician Contribution to Risk Reduction?

Richard L. Doyle, M.D.

Aligning Clinical Practice with Aggregate Managed Care Goals

Increasing the hospital's degree of health care management will not go smoothly without the buy in of physicians and administration. This buy-in should be considered in planning the integrated system, developing practice guidelines, implementing the efficiency measures, evaluating the financial structure, assessing potential partners, and using the results of the reporting system to modify practices. The practitioners who provide for individual patients ultimately determine the success of accepting managed care risk. This chapter addresses the development of optimal practices as well as analyzing performance against appropriate benchmarks.

Using the actuarial analysis outlined in chapters 2 and 3, a health care organization can develop a model for the aggregate performance needed to bear the risks under a managed care contract. Table 5-1 illustrates aggregate goals that emerge from this analysis. However, these aggregate goals are only the first step for defining specifically what clinicians can do to contribute to efficient organizational performance. The health care organization must move from aggregate to individual performance goals to ensure that individual practitioners contribute to the management of risk.

In identifying what will be meaningful to clinicians, we will use two constructs—aggregate targets and individual best practice goals. The term *aggregate targets* is used to mean objective facts derived from a data source identi-

Table 5-1. Sample Aggregate Utilization Goals

Population Served	Bed Days per 1,000 Aggregate Goal	Average LOS Aggregate Goal
Commercial	Under 200	Near 3.0
Medicare	Under 1,000	Near 5.0
Typical mix of commercial and Medicare	About 300	Under 4.0

fied by the health care organization. For example, Milliman & Robertson data show that very efficient hospitals achieve an average length of stay (ALOS) of 1.3 days for vaginal deliveries. A health care organization could set this aggregate target to evaluate its own utilization. The term *best practice goals* is used to mean targets developed by practitioners in a given clinical area that, in their subjective judgment, are optimal for uncomplicated cases. For example, the system may set a one-day LOS as the best practice goal for uncomplicated vaginal deliveries (given appropriate home care services). At this point, it should be noted the term *best practice* is being used in a narrower sense than many clinicians are used to. It is used here as an adjective because the goal would be an aspect of what constitutes best practice; its usage it as a noun would embrace all aspects of a clinical process. Readers should not read into this usage that we define *best practice* solely in terms of LOS. The impact that best practice goals have on aggregate targets is described later in this chapter.

A health care organization must identify *clinically relevant* aggregate targets and develop best practice goals in conjunction with physicians and others involved in patient care, drawing on both internal and external sources of data and readily available practice parameters. Some sources for guidelines are identified in the additional resources section at the end of this publication. For success in securing managed care business, the organization also must create systems for analyzing what *best practice* yields in terms of aggregate target performance or incremental improvement toward the aggregate target.

Finding a productive approach to identifying aggregate targets, developing goals, and creating systems that ensure best practice will challenge both administrators and clinical staff. This chapter describes the authors' approach, which balances the realities of how managed care organizations evaluate the relative attractiveness of potential partners and the concerns of clinical staff.

The first step in the process of identifying aggregate targets is to define what the targets are meant to represent. Unfortunately, traditional utilization targets have tended to be:

- Thresholds (usually stated in terms of a standard deviation from a statistical average)

- Historical averages
- Modes of performance across the community
- Relative percentile ranking in comparison to other providers

Such utilization targets will not drive significant performance improvement. Rather, they lead to developing strategies to avoid the least favorable of traditional results. This in turn leads to ratifying traditional practice patterns rather than seeking more efficient approaches.

More useful aggregate targets and best practice goals may be derived by first defining groups of patients who will be targeted. The groups targeted should be based on current and projected patient mix, with priorities set reflecting volume, cost, and risk. Organizations ultimately will want to create strategies for all populations (as, for example, for both Medicare and commercially insured populations and for both low-risk, uncomplicated DRGs and high-risk DRGs with high costs per discharge). For several reasons, we believe systems should first focus the clinical efficiency improvement process on commercially insured populations in DRGs with minimal risk of complications. First, for reasons explained below, this population will involve clinical decision making that is less open to disagreement, and those involved in developing best practices may thus achieve consensus within a relatively short time frame. In addition, system inefficiencies identified in these minimal-risk DRGs are likely to be generalizable across the system. That is, the organization may achieve some quick results with far-reaching positive consequences.

More important, uncomplicated patients represent, for most systems, the largest single clinical risk class of patients in the commercially insured population. Eighty percent of patients with commercial coverage are in minimal-risk DRGs for which adverse outcomes occur less than 1 percent of the time. Thus, this category of patients serves as the closest to an ideal base for clinical goal or guideline development.

Because most physicians are not trained to analyze patients by risk class, planning optimal protocols should begin with a limited number of respected practitioners. Institutions relying on limited practitioner panels for initial draft plans have achieved excellent results. The practitioner(s) drafting the plan should be provided data outlining aggressive aggregate targets and information on best practice, including the best practices from other delivery systems. (Several sources for this information are noted in the additional resources at the end of this publication.)

Those responsible for the clinical management initiative should then circulate the draft protocols and implementation plans to:

- Other medical practitioners
- Quality management and case management staff
- Acute care nursing
- Support services (such as physical therapy, rehabilitation, and home health)

The clinical management team should lead this process and keep in mind that large meetings are less likely to reach rapid consensus. At each meeting, clinical management must seek honest feedback but emphasize that the objective is improved efficiency in the use of resources needed for the patients in the uncomplicated risk class. During the meetings, clinical management should ask not only "Why can't we fulfill this draft plan a significant percentage of the time?" but also "Is there any possibility that a *more* efficient plan could be delivered some of the time?" This consensus process should result in plans for efficiency that both receive support from individual medical practitioners and promote clinical practice that is as expeditious as practically achievable.

To illustrate this process, following is a description of one client's experience in examining cesarean sections in a community where the traditional LOS was four postpartum days. An obstetrics/family practice/pediatric task force reviewed a postpartum timetable for uncomplicated patients:

- *Postpartum day 1:* Offering a diet, discontinuance of intravenous feedings, and substitution of oral for parenteral pain management
- *Postpartum day 2:* Oral medications, an advanced diet in an afebrile ambulatory patient who will be discharged on the second postpartum day

This sequence of care was thought to define favorable and efficient practice. Further discussion across the broader group of practitioners resulted in the adoption of the following protocol:

- *Postpartum day 1:* Offering of liquids
- *Postpartum day 2:* Discontinuance of intravenous feeding and parenteral medication
- *Postpartum day 3:* Discharge of the afebrile ambulatory patient on an advanced diet and oral medication

After this plan was adopted, the client's system achieved a mode LOS for C-sections of 3 days, and the ALOS decreased from 4.3 to 3.2 days. Clinical management had changed a practice pattern with a high degree of predictability and had moved the system toward efficiency. As illustrated in this example, explicit inpatient care plans should define day-by-day sequences of care and recovery, with an LOS goal and defined appropriate times for levels of care and *major* ancillary services.

Though this chapter emphasizes goals based on LOS, health systems should establish similar goals for admission rates as well. The development of outpatient surgery provides significant opportunities for avoiding inpatient surgical admissions. In many hospitals, opportunities exist for protocols focused on avoiding inappropriate nonsurgical admits through home care and active holding beds associated with a hospital or other outpatient facility.

Tables 5-2, 5-3, and 5-4 illustrate some possible outcomes of the goal-

Table 5-2. Goal Setting for Admission Rates for Selected Clinical Events

Clinical Event	Portion of Admits	
	Traditional Average	Aggregate Target
C-section rate	25%	10%
Percentage of chemical dependency rehabilitation as inpatient	50%	5%

setting process. Table 5-2 compares admission rates expressed as traditional averages and as more meaningful aggregate targets set by the organization. Table 5-3 (p. 48) compares LOS for six clinical groups expressed as a traditional average, an aggregate target for the total population within the group, and the shortest observed LOS (a best practice outcome). This table illustrates the effect of complicated patients on averages (the difference between the aggregate target for a specified population and the best practice goal for individual patients). It also suggests the cost-savings resulting if clinicians and administration set aside traditional averages and focus on the clinical process that achieves best practice outcomes. Table 5-4 (p. 49) illustrates aggregate targets for care.

We believe that best practices for best recovery or best maintenance of health (that is, best patient care outcomes) require clinical protocols that incorporate objectives for efficiency. A successful planning process will moderate some practitioners' misgivings about focusing on the uncomplicated risk class, as well as identifying potential obstacles to efficiency.

Acknowledging the Concerns of Clinical Staff

Before working with physicians and other clinical staff in setting aggregate targets or best practice goals, health care administrators should consider the concerns of clinicians, including:

- *Focus on most memorable patients:* An individual clinician's top-of-mind recollection usually is of the most memorable, sickest patients. Goal setting should not be guided by worst cases, but their existence should be acknowledged.
- *Focus on the Medicare population:* Hospital-based clinical management has encouraged a focus on cost-control strategies for the Medicare population and the risks associated with DRG-based payments

Table 5-3. Goal Setting for Length of Stay for Selected Clinical Events

Clinical Event	LOS in Days		
	Traditional Average	Aggregate Target (Average for Population)	Best Practice (for Individuals)
Vaginal delivery	2.1	1.3	1
C-section	4.3	2.3	2
Heart surgery	9.9	6.1	3
Major joint surgery	7.3	5.0	3
Medical respiratory case	4.8	2.7	1
Stroke	8.6	5.0	2

for this population. Providers now need to consider the risk characteristics of managed health care groups and create strategies based on patient mix as well as payer mix. This probably means that the aggregate targets will be for groups that are less complex clinically than the Medicare population. However, managed care reimbursement may be more restrictive than Medicare and may require utilization management strategies that aim at achieving greater efficiency.

- *Perceptions of what constitutes "best practice":* Health care providers are developing approaches for achieving excellence under such banners as total quality management, continuous quality improvement, and process reengineering. The champions of these approaches may not view the approach outlined in this chapter as consistent with their preferred approach. For example, in defining best practice, they may prefer sophisticated clinical practice parameters, clinical guidelines developed by medical specialty associations, and clinical pathways. Despite the value of clinical pathways, their development is a lengthy and complex process. In addition, pathways may cover all possible complications (however infrequent) with all ancillary services noted in more detail than is necessary for achieving optimal clinical efficiency. Administration must nonetheless pursue the difficult objective of achieving efficiency with the large uncomplicated group.

- *Interdependence on hospital-provided services:* The entire burden for improving efficiency, including reducing LOS, should not fall on physicians. We have observed that approximately 20 percent of avoidable hospital days occur because of delays in needed hospital-provided services. Such delays could occur because of either the unavailability of certain services at certain times or the inability to secure timely physician decisions and approvals. By definition, day-by-day practice is

Table 5-4. Goal Setting for Outpatient Services

Clinical Event	Traditional Average	Aggregate Target
Office visits (primary and specialty care)	4,500	3,560
Radiology	700	400
Pathology	2,200	1,200
Prescriptions	4,100	3,000
Total	11,600	8,200

independent of weekends or time of day—for both hospitals and physicians. Systems need to make available many decisive diagnostic, therapeutic, and administrative services when they will have the greatest impact on efficiency.

Dramatic improvements, often through fairly simple adjustments in practice, become obvious only when physicians, nurse managers, and others can share the effects they experience from the actions of others. To get physicians involved in what they perceive to be the hospital's problems, focus the search on what is best for the physicians' patients rather than allowing discussion to focus on what is best or most convenient for hospital staff.

- *Fear of potential staff reductions:* Improving the efficiency of patient care commonly involves a reexamination of the work and roles of the providers involved. This reexamination frequently shifts responsibility from more costly sites and personnel to sites and personnel that can be shown to achieve the desired outcomes more cost-effectively. Physicians, nurses, therapists, technicians, and pharmacists, among others, may resist participating in a process that results in downsizing. Resistance also may surface relating to perceptions of the quality of service in alternative settings or the professional competence of less highly paid personnel. For example, acute care nursing may resist transferring patient education to the more cost-effective outpatient setting, because of both the resulting reduction in nursing staff and the perception that vital functions will not be handled well.

- *Fear of failure to meet ambitious goals:* In the our experience, physicians are most comfortable with goals they can be assured of achieving at least 90 percent of the time and may resist actuarially established targets. They also may view the best practice goal as the LOS that the network expects them to achieve 90 percent of the time and voice resistance when this goal is significantly below the aggregate target for the population as a whole (as is the case with four of the six clinical events shown in table 5-3). They may believe that the network is placing unrealistic expectations on them and making little room for the exercise of case-by-case judgment. They also may voice concern that the network will use LOS and only LOS to make qualitative judgments about their competence. Payers will likely expect best practice to become the mode (most frequent event). However, payers will recognize that because of complications, 10 to 20 percent of the cases may not meet best practice targets and that adverse case mix may cause an even higher proportion of exceptions.

Using Actuarial Cost Models in Setting Priorities for Goal Setting

Table 5-5 shows the distribution of costs by category for a population of commercially insured beneficiaries under age 65 (excluding dental expenses) based on an actuarial cost model for unmanaged care (such as the one shown as table 2-1 in chapter 2). This breakdown suggests where the potential for the most significant cost savings lies. However, these data must be used with some care because they may poorly suit particular health care delivery systems. As discussed in chapters 2 and 3, the actuarial model developed for a specific organization may indicate a different prioritization depending on the scope of services provided, population served, and current clinical efficiency. The percentages shown below correspond to a relatively rich benefit design that includes coverage for behavioral health, physical exams, and vision.

Acknowledging that each system must be evaluated individually, table 5-5 suggests the following first cut at setting priorities and developing strategies:

- *Inpatient facility costs:* About 34 percent of the total health care dollar for commercially insured patients.
  — Reducing inpatient LOS
  — Avoiding unscheduled admissions, usually nonsurgical, by using appropriate outpatient services or active holding beds for brief periods
  — Implementing case management for patients with chronic conditions so that they receive higher-quality, cost-effective care with the best achievable health status in the least restrictive setting
- *Outpatient facility costs:* About 12 percent of the total health care dollar for commercially insured patients, but the second priority because outpatient facility costs are closely linked to inpatient facility costs— for both payers and providers. Some health care systems find that outpatient utilization relates inversely to inpatient utilization; although total costs become lower, utilization of nonhospital services (such as physician, long-term care, and home health care) may increase.
  — Performing surgery on an outpatient basis as often as possible; making full use of the facility (about five surgeries per eight-hour day)

Table 5-5. Approximate Portion of Health Care Dollar for Commercially Insured Population under Age 65, Unmanaged Care System

Cost Category	%
Inpatient hospital	34
Outpatient hospital	12
Specialist physician	32
Primary care physician	10
Outpatient prescription drugs	8
Miscellaneous	4

through (1) short operating times through efficient surgery management and (2) short recovery times through skillful anesthesia

— Avoiding unnecessary emergency department utilization through improved access to non-hospital-based ambulatory care

- *Specialist costs:* About 32 percent of the total health care dollar for commercially insured patients.

— Educating primary care physicians (PCPs) about comprehensive services, which will reduce specialist costs

— Planning for the appropriate use of specialists (rather than PCPs) for procedures and consultations and for ongoing care when the specialist appears to be qualitatively the best choice and to offer the most efficient approach

- *Primary care physicians (PCPs):* About 10 percent of the total health care dollar for commercially insured patients. Under gatekeeper models, PCPs can influence all other cost categories, sometimes significantly.

— Including incentives to PCPs to perform nearly comprehensive services instead of maximizing referrals to specialists

- *Outpatient prescription drugs:* About 8 percent of the total health care dollar for commercially insured patients.

— Practicing pharmacy management to avoid nonindicated antibiotic prescriptions; to encourage use of generic or less expensive but efficient drugs; to avoid unnecessary multiple prescriptions; and to increase patient compliance

- *Miscellaneous categories:* An assortment of other categories of care comprise the remaining 4 percent. These include vision care, podiatric care, speech therapy, prosthetics, durable medical equipment, ambulance service, and the like.

Chapter 6

What Role and Risk Will You Assume?

Howard A. Levin, M.D.

Providers can assume risk under a variety of roles. In this chapter, these roles are described as:

- *Partner in a provider network:* Hospitals, physicians, or ancillary services providing a defined service or set of services as part of a larger network
- *Integrator of a full-service provider network:* Hospitals, physician groups, or managed care organizations providing the full range of health care services, whether through ownership of the necessary provider organizations or through subcontracting
- *Owner/operator of a provider/insurer organization:* Hospitals, physicians, managed care organizations, or insurers not only providing a vertically integrated health care delivery system but also owning the insurance product under which services are provided

This simple continuum of roles illustrates a graduated scale of risk assumption moving from the most limited risk of a contracting partner to the greatest risk of being both provider and insurer. Providers may not find themselves playing only one of the roles described above. For example, a hospital or multispecialty group practice may participate in a regional cardiovascular service network (a contracting partner in a larger network) and also contract with an HMO to provide a full range of services (an integrator of the HMO's provider network).

Even the term *integrator* will have different meanings to different readers of this publication, depending on their vision of who needs to come together within a health care system. This chapter focuses on the risk-bearing providers in an integrated delivery system to identify the capabilities needed to successfully manage risk.

Whatever level of risk they choose to assume, providers will be at risk for not only the cost but also the quality of care provided. Quality management is becoming an increasingly important function for both the provider of care and

53

the integrated health care system. Payers are demanding objective standards to determine the quality of the system. Additionally, as the market continues to develop, the customers of HMOs and insurance companies are going to demand evidence of the value of the products. They will want to know how good a product they will get for their dollars.

Quality management organizations are attempting to define a core set of performance measures (with standardized definitions and specific methodologies for deriving measures), most notably the National Committee for Quality Assurance (NCQA) in its Health Plan Employer Data and Information Set (HEDIS). At a minimum, providers should collect sufficient information to address the HEDIS measures. Developed organizations will be expected to be able to manage the quality as well as the utilization of care.

Risks of Partners in Provider Networks

Hospitals, physicians, and ancillary service providers entering into managed care relationships accept risk in the forms described in chapter 3 and evaluate benefits along the lines described in chapters 2 and 4. Though operating in a managed care environment implies a reorientation of management and clinical staff, partnership may not require all insurer functions. Essentially, those entering into a partnership must address two questions:

- Can you manage the risk?
- Are you holding only part of the solution?

Though not currently common, there is the potential that partnerships can evolve into exclusive relationships that fully commit the provider. Making a commitment to any exclusive network means more than a review of the contract and actuarial analysis of financial risk. It involves a due diligence review of the entire organization—its value, competitive position, cost-effectiveness, and management. Becoming a part of a system also often requires a capital investment, adding a new dimension to the provider's risk.

Can You Manage the Risk?

You must be able to manage the risk that you have acquired and ensure that you are not accountable for costs of services over which you have no control. For example, in a capitated radiology contract, there is potentially very little ability to manage the risk, other than decreasing the unit cost through reduction in underlying costs. Tests are ordered not by the radiologist (who holds the risk) but, rather, by the physician. To manage the risk, the radiologist could, among other things, require access to the ordering physicians and to active participation in developing guidelines for ordering tests. The radiologist also could insist that the payer structure incentives for physicians to follow those guidelines.

As described in chapter 3, a hospital can acquire risk in a number of ways. Capitation, per diem, and performance-based contracts—or some combination of these—represent the most common. Under a capitation contract, hospital ability to manage risk is limited in that the physician orders hospital services. With this risk, a hospital should develop strong management capability to direct and incent admitting physicians toward efficiency in their admissions, use of inpatient ancillary services, and lengths of stay. The best solution to developing these capabilities is to involve all parties early in planning risk management procedures and incentives.

Are You Holding Only Part of the Solution?

Risk contracts for specific services create the possibility for misaligned incentives. For example, a network or insurance company could strictly manage access to home care. Under a capitated or DRG-based payment, a payer could require a hospital provider to perform the services that a home care agency could otherwise deliver, adding costs for the provider but not the payer. This risk is addressed by ensuring that the hospital's contract includes financing for alternative care services.

Flat per diem contracts also tend to create problems in the incentives between the hospital that buys the risk and the insurance company. As mentioned in previous chapters, a hospital stay usually costs the most the first day and the least the last day. The insurance company and the hospital usually anticipate a certain length of stay (LOS) to determine the acceptable per diem. However, the insurance company or the HMO may then enlist the hospital and physicians in markedly reducing LOS. The result could be a shorter LOS, increasing the portion of high-cost days and resulting in a possible loss for the hospital. Per diem rates must reflect the chance that efficiency will reduce revenues; performance incentives in the contract reduce this risk.

Risks of Integrators of Full-Service Provider Networks

The contract between a network provider/integrator and an insurer may have the integrator responsible for all medical services and the insurer responsible for all administrative and marketing services. Under such an arrangement, the integrator may retain as much as 85 percent of the premium. In this type of arrangement, the insurer essentially moves the risk of all health care costs to the integrator, who may in turn strike subcapitated contracts with other components of the necessary provider network (as, for example, behavioral health services providers). The network integrator thus functions as an insurer with respect to health care risk.

Contracting to supply a full continuum of services presents both advantages and risks. A key advantage is the network's ability to look at the entire spectrum of care and to choose the most cost-effective modality to produce the desired outcome. Those integrators who can effectively manage all care and who can document the network's achievement of the highest-quality, most cost-effective care across a wide geographic area will be most competitive.

Coordinating multiple providers involves negotiating alliances and long-term contractual obligations. It could also require significant capital for the acquisition of physician practices and investment in sophisticated management and clinical information systems. The required considerable investment in information systems technology is part of the organization's assets (with acquired value) and may help position the network to be the most attractive partner for insurers (whose systems are likely to be more limited in scope and capability).

Integrators also need the expertise of specialized personnel, including actuaries with managed care experience, medical directors with managed care experience, management information systems developers with a knowledge of community health information network (CHIN) technology, and legal counsel with expertise in managed care contracting. Qualified professionals currently are in short supply and will not easily be recruited away from well-established managed care organizations. The payback for investment in technology and personnel can be considerable, as evidenced by the success of organizations such as the Mullikin Medical Group in California, which has gained an increasingly stronger position in its relationships with several HMOs.

A basic challenge for integrators of full-service provider networks is that of developing hospital–physician integration strategies that yield a shared understanding of managed care goals and that align hospital and physician financial incentives. A variety of approaches to hospital–physician integration are evolving, including physician–hospital organizations (PHOs), medical service organizations (MSOs), and medical foundations, among others. It is beyond the scope of this publication to describe all the issues involved; readers should refer to *Hospital–Physician Integration* or other materials listed in the additional resources at the end of this publication as well as successful peers.

Risk issues for integrators of full-service networks relate to:

- Underwriting
- Benefit levels
- Actuarial estimate of expected costs
- Health care delivery system management

Underwriting

If the network assumes all the risk, the insurance company may not carefully evaluate potential risks in the enrolled group. Thus, the network should evaluate the potential that the insurer will attract a high portion of high-risk individuals—and pass the risk on to the network. Additionally, the experience of groups should be routinely assessed to ensure that renewal terms are appropriate.

Benefit Levels

Many insurers now offer multiple benefit plans and plan limitations. In such cases, it is important to identify each plan and its benefits to properly assess overall risk. Though patient cost sharing generally reduces cost, high out-of-pocket costs present the risk that the member might not be able to make the payments and the provider will absorb the risk that it cannot collect copays and deductibles. When examining benefit plans, careful calculations must be made, preferably with the help of a competent actuary.

Actuarial Estimate of Expected Costs

Actuaries usually estimate future expenses based on historical utilization and cost for each service, considering factors such as the number, age, sex, and economic class of insured members; the plan's benefit level; general economic conditions and trends; and so on. The costs usually are divided into different services and expressed as utilization, average price, and costs per member per month (PMPM) or year. Before accepting any level of payment, a health system should determine its expected level of costs to determine whether its revenue will at least meet its expected costs. (See chapters 2 and 4 for examples of these kinds of calculations using actuarial models.)

Experiments have begun with an additional method of evaluating costs. This new area is *disease management* or *demand management,* which tries to determine the cost for treating or preventing each type of medical problem. Risk thus becomes epidemiologically based on age- and sex-adjusted incidence and prevalence of disease. (For example, type II diabetes has a prevalence of X per 1,000 adjusted for the age of the population expected to be insured.) Provider familiarity with this approach is necessary as insurers become more sophisticated in pricing.

Health Care Delivery System Management

Successful management of a health care delivery system relies on the effective management of physicians and providers and efficient management of patients and their medical care.

Provider Network Management

The crucial ingredient for network integrator success is sophisticated management with a vision that enlists the cooperation of health care providers and other personnel within the network. The network integrator must have the discipline to select the right providers and the leadership and incentives to motivate them to carry out the network's goals.

Effective communication with the network of physicians and other providers will be essential to successfully managing the network. Administrative issues such as what benefits are covered and how each benefit plan works will need to be made clear to each provider and its office staff. Telephone lines must be manned to respond to questions quickly and effectively when a provider calls its contact with the plan.

Patient Care Management

The increased risk associated with fixed payment for services demands an aggressive approach to keeping costs for care on target. Active oversight of the use of costly resources should be the objective of an effective patient management department. The department should provide precertification, concurrent review, case management, and retrospective review. All potential decision makers (physicians in particular) should be educated in appropriately employing resources. Benchmarking against a known efficient style of practice is an effective part of education programs. (See chapter 5.)

A major strength of an integrated network is the capacity to redeploy resources to increase efficiency. This includes the appropriate use of home care alternatives to inpatient stays and newer concepts such as disease management. Under disease management, budgets may be developed for illnesses such as diabetes. The directors of this budget then decide the most efficient way to produce the best outcomes of care, which likely include preventive care services, such as nutrition counseling and exercise programs. Such preventive care services also may decrease the need for expensive inpatient care for more severe cases such as ketoacidosis and coma and, over time, the complications of diabetes such as vascular disease. If an integrated health care network can move resources from the hospital setting to the outpatient and health education settings, better disease management may result.

Risks of Owner/Operators of Provider/ Insurer Organizations

Some providers with insurance or HMO functions have been extraordinarily successful (as, for example, Kaiser Permanente), but there also have been failures of provider-owned HMOs or insurance companies. A direct link between provider and insurer may reduce the risk of losing patients but may create additional risks and responsibilities. Running an insurance function involves new expertise, including:

- Capital management
- Marketing and member relations
- Actuarial skills
- Payment administration
- Benefit plan design
- Management information systems
- Provider relations and contracting
- Compliance with state insurance requirements

Capital Management

Capital requirements for start-up could easily reach five to ten million dollars to cover the cost of network development, market research, and the initial period of negative cash flow during the time the business is recruiting enough membership to cover its operating costs. In addition, state insurance departments may impose minimum capital requirements and actuarial projections demonstrating compliance.

There are a number of methods to raise capital, including allowing investments by physicians, developing a consortium of hospitals and providers, and if the organization is a for-profit entity, going to capital markets and venture capitalists. With these methods, the price for sharing risk often is loss of control and less of a share of the profits. Before considering any financial arrangements among providers, competent legal counsel should examine potential antitrust or fraud and abuse issues and formulate an appropriate structure.

Marketing and Member Relations

Although combined provider–insurer operations reduce the risk of losing patients, provider–insurers do acquire the risk of enrolling members. As with any business, telling your story is a critical aspect for the success of being an HMO or insurer. Your investment in systems, personnel, buildings, and other administrative expenses now must be protected by ensuring that existing membership is retained and new membership comes in the door. The risk of loss of membership and market share is much more significant for you as an insurer than for a hospital provider holding contracts with several HMOs who trade membership from time to time.

Managed care marketing for an integrated health care delivery network requires different skills than used in a traditional hospital. The company will need to be "sold" to providers, employees, and employers (as well as investors if the company is for-profit with capital obtained through outside sources).

If the risks are to be managed, appropriate marketing expertise must be added through consultants, dedicated employees, or contract service groups. The skills required include strategic business analysis, sales incentive and management functions, advertising, and public relations.

The target market is also new for hospitals. Selling to customers such as employee benefit executives, insurance brokers, and company CEOs and CFOs require new approaches based on good benefits, price, perceived network quality, and excellent customer service. Those hospitals with experience in marketing occupational health services to employers will have some advanced understanding of these differences.

Repeat business is the most important area in any customer mix. Keeping close contact with all your members and employees, particularly the well ones through wellness programs and health newsletters, is very important for renewal enrollment and risk management. Satisfaction surveys and focus groups are useful in making sure you are appropriately managing this part of your business. In addition, ongoing contact with employers through account representatives will ensure that you are meeting employer needs.

Actuarial Skills

As demonstrated in chapter 2, developing and running an insurance company or HMO means acquiring new financial risk for actual health care costs. The owner/operator of an integrated delivery system that includes insurance functions needs actuarial evaluations of risk for a number of purposes—but especially for determining premiums and the organization's financial status. In the current environment, this evaluation has become even more expensive because of customer demand for unique products, such as those with point-of-service programs, varying copays, deductibles, and benefit levels or those directed at Medicare, Medicaid, or CHAMPUS. Your actuary, whether a consultant or an employee, must estimate the costs of each of these programs and develop premiums that are profitable and competitive. In addition, many state's regulators require actuarial certification of rates and financial status.

Determining whether the network has made or lost money overall or on any particular contract also requires actuarial evaluation. This is because accrual accounting requires evaluation of contingent income and expenses that involve risk, and the corresponding assets and liabilities. In insurance companies, these are actuarial functions.

Payment Administration

As an insurer, you become a payer of providers and insurance claims. The standard issues that must be addressed are quick turnaround times to please your providers and contract administration to ensure that payment is at contracted rates. You also will need systems to evaluate the payment accuracy and to detect fraud, as well as practices such as unbundling of services and linkage with a patient management function to ensure that payment is only for approved services. In addition, efficient claims service is a key member satisfaction issue that affects retention and marketing.

Benefit Plan Design

Insurance services for employers, government programs, and individuals require products that answer the specific needs of these groups. Whereas, in the past a single HMO product was all that was needed to enter the marketplace, today the purchasers of insurance are demanding benefit plans with multiple levels of copays, coinsurance, and out-of-pocket maximums, in addition to point-of-service programs. Many large employers now are using HMO networks as a PPO or a self-insured HMO. In these programs, the employers carry the risk while the HMO charges a service fee to provide and manage the network. Increasing buyer demands for new products in the marketplace will challenge the design and product management capabilities of providers new to the insurer business.

Management Information Systems

Unless you can monitor what is happening in your integrated system, you cannot manage the system effectively. Electronic data systems will be essential to tie the pieces together and form the basis for rational strategic and operational decision making. The ultimate information system would interconnect all the parties in the network and provide the following capabilities:

- *Administrative and financial functions:* Health plan coverage verification, claims processing, payment processing (including electronic data interchange), materials management (including electronic purchase orders, receipts, and pricing updates), and performance monitoring (as described in chapter 3)
- *Clinical management functions:* Data storage and retrieval systems that enable analysis of cost, utilization, outcomes, and quality measurements; clinical decision support, perhaps including electronic access to test results; a computer-based patient record (CPR); drug formulary; directory of referral resources; electronic mail for providing updates on new medical procedures, drugs, biomedical devices, and clinical protocols, as well as providing for on-line consults; and patient scheduling and tracking mechanisms

Currently, no single vendor can fulfill these and other visionary expectations (such as telemedicine capabilities). Provider–insurer organizations will need to decide early on whether to invest in building their own systems or to purchase and interconnect vendor-owned systems.

Provider Relations and Contracting

The provider–insurer organization will have to be skilled in negotiating and managing contractual relationships. Contracting demands the ability to assess and monitor the performance of these contracted services. Additionally, management systems will have to be in place to effect the smooth flow of referrals and patients across the various providers. Electronic links would help large systems function efficiently.

Compliance with State Insurance Requirements

Insuring the risk for health care costs opens you to the scrutiny of state insurance regulators. One of their main interests is to serve the public interest by ensuring financial solvency and stability, including claims-paying ability. This means that you will have to assess the requirements of relevant regulations and sound management practices through appropriate counsel and maintain the required reserves.

Additional Resources

Actuarial Issues

Davidoff, D. S., and Pyenson, B. Actuarial issues in play-or-pay. Research report. Milliman & Robertson, June 1992.

Hauboldt, R., Hauser, P., and Litow, M. E. Adverse selection in health care. Research report. Milliman & Robertson, June 1994.

Hauboldt, R., Hauser, P., and Litow, M. E. Cost implications of human organ transplantations, an update: 1993. Research report. Milliman & Robertson, Feb. 1993.

Society of Actuaries. Effects of resource based RVS in Medicare on private health insurance. *Record* 18(1A), 1992.

Society of Actuaries. Health care management. *Record* 13(1), 1987.

Society of Actuaries. Internal rate of return as an evaluator of tax-planning strategies. *Transactions* XLIV, 1992.

Society of Actuaries. The practical application of risk analysis techniques in health insurance. *Record* 9(4), 1983.

Society of Actuaries. *Study Note 520-22-89, Summary of Cost Containment Programs.* Schaumburg, IL: SOA, 1989.

Society of Actuaries. *Study Note 520-40-89, Financial Reporting Issues for Alternative Healthcare Delivery Systems.* Schaumburg, IL: SOA, 1989.

Society of Actuaries. *Study Note 520-42-92, Alternate Delivery Systems Corporate Management.* Schaumburg, IL: SOA, 1992.

Note: Reports published by Milliman & Robertson, Inc., are available from local Milliman & Robertson offices.

Society of Actuaries. *Study Note 520-43-94, Monitoring and Projecting Pricing Trends in a Managed Care Environment.* Schaumburg, IL: SOA, 1994.

Society of Actuaries. *Study Note 520-44-94, American Institute of Certified Public Accountants Financial Accounting and Reporting by Providers of Prepaid Health Care Services.* Schaumburg, IL: SOA, 1994.

Sutton, H. L., Jr., and Sorbo, A. J., editors. *Actuarial Issues in the Fee for Service/Prepaid Medical Group.* 2nd ed. Denver, CO: Center for Research in Ambulatory Health Care Administration, Medical Group Management Association, 1993.

Contracting

Axene, D. V., and Doyle, R. Financial evaluation of healthcare provider contracts. Research report. Milliman & Robertson, Apr. 1992.

Data Sources

Doyle, R. L. *Healthcare Management Guidelines.* Vol. 1. *Inpatient and Surgical Care.* Milliman & Robertson, Oct. 1994.

Doyle, R. L. *Healthcare Management Guidelines.* Vol. 2. *Return-to-Work Planning.* Milliman & Robertson, Jan. 1994.

Doyle, R. L., and Feren, A. P. *Healthcare Management Guidelines.* Vol. 3. *Ambulatory Care Guidelines.* Milliman & Robertson, Jan. 1994.

Doyle, R. L., Pinney, M. H., and Spong, F. W. *Healthcare Management Guidelines.* Vol. 4. *Home Care and Case Management.* Milliman & Robertson, June 1994.

Fry, J. D., and Young, R. W. *The Health Care Data Source Book: Finding the Right Information and Making the Most of It.* Chicago: American Hospital Publishing, 1992. [Second edition in press for publication late 1995.]

Stepnick, L., editor. *Outcomes Strategy: Measurement of Hospital Quality under Reform.* Washington, DC: Health Care Advisory Board, 1993.

Toepp, M. C., and Kuznets, N., editors. *Directory of Practices Parameters: Titles, Sources, and Updates.* Chicago: American Medical Association, 1993.

Insurance Practices

Actuarial Standards Board. *Actuarial Standard Practice No. 5: Insurance Health Claim Liabilities.* Washington, DC: ASB, 1991.

Bluhm, W. F., editor. *Group Insurance.* Winsted, CT: ACTEX Publications, 1992.

Herrle, G. N., and Alexander, R. D. Considerations in the design of open-ended HMO products. Research report. Milliman & Robertson, July 1990.

Herrle, G. N. Preferred Provider Organizations. Research report. Milliman & Robertson, Aug. 1986.

Melek, S. P. Mental health care reform—can everyone win? Research report. Milliman & Robertson, Oct. 1993.

Ogden, D. Healthcare systems: health maintenance organizations. Research report. Milliman & Robertson, Feb. 1987.

Pollock, W. M., and Ogden, D. F. Small group market reform: new opportunities for HMOs. Research report. Milliman & Robertson, June 1991.

Rosenbloom, J. S., and Hallman, G., editors. *Employee Benefit Planning.* 3rd ed. Des Moines, IA: Prentice-Hall Paramount Publishing, 1991.

Snook, T. D. NAIC small group health model law: premium rates and renewability of coverage for health insurance sold to the small groups. Research report. Milliman & Robertson, Apr. 1991.

Society of Actuaries. Experience rating and credibility in group health insurance. *Record* 18(1B), 1992.

Society of Actuaries. Prescription drug plans. *Record* 15(1), 1989.

Society of Actuaries. *Study Note 320-32-88, Underwriting Group Insurance.* Schaumburg, IL: SOA, 1988.

Society of Actuaries. *Study Note 320-38-88, Coordination of Benefits in Group Health Insurance.* Schaumburg, IL: SOA, 1988.

Society of Actuaries. *Study Note 422-25-91, Causes and Effects of Inflationary Trends in Group Insurance Pricing.* Schaumburg, IL: SOA, 1991.

Society of Actuaries. *Study Note 520-37-91, Marketing Issues for Alternative Healthcare Delivery Systems.* Schaumburg, IL: SOA, 1991.

Society of Actuaries. *Study Note 520-38-91, Underwriting Issues for Alternative Healthcare Delivery Systems.* Schaumburg, IL: SOA, 1991.

Society of Actuaries. *Study Note 520-42-92, Actuarial Standards Board No. 16: Concerning Health Maintenance Organizations and Other Managed Care Health Plans.* Schaumburg, IL: SOA, 1992.

Society of Actuaries. *Study Note 422-39-94, Variation by Duration in Small Group Medical Insurance Claims.* Schaumburg, IL: SOA, 1994.

Whitney, E. L., and Dunlap, J.A. Effective risk sharing under a point-of-service program. Research report. Milliman & Robertson, June 1993.

Whitney, E. L., and Finch, W. E. Pricing the open ended HMO. Research report. Milliman & Robertson, May 1991.

Patient Care Management

Axene, D. V., and Doyle, R. Analysis of medically unnecessary inpatient services. Research Report. Milliman & Robertson, July 1994.

Donovan, M. R., and Matson, T. A., editors. *Outpatient Case Management: Strategies for a New Reality.* Chicago: American Hospital Publishing, 1994.

Spath, P. L., editor. *Clinical Paths: Tools for Outcomes Management.* Chicago: American Hospital Publishing, 1994.

Zander, K., editor for The Center for Case Management. *Managing Outcomes through Collaborative Care: The Application of CareMapping and Case Management.* Chicago, IL: American Hospital Publishing, 1995.

Quality Management

Benson, D. S. *Measuring Outcomes in Ambulatory Care.* Chicago: American Hospital Publishing, 1992.

Ciccone, K. R., and Lord, J. T., for the Hospital Association of New York State. *IQA-2: Continuous Quality Improvement through Integrated Quality Assessment.* Chicago: American Hospital Publishing, 1992.

Gift, R. G., and Mosel, D. *Benchmarking in Health Care: Collaborative Approach.* Chicago: American Hospital Publishing, 1994.

Satinsky, M. A. *An Executive Guide to Case Management Strategies.* Chicago: American Hospital Publishing, 1995.

Reform and Environmental Impact

Dymowski, R. J., and Pyenson, B. Will it work? Evaluating health care reform. Research report. Milliman & Robertson, Nov. 1992.

Employee Benefit Research Institute. *Medicare Reform: The Private Sector Impact.* Washington, DC: EBRI, 1985.

Employee Benefit Research Institute. *The Changing Health Care Market.* Edited by F. B. McArdle. Washington, DC: EBRI, 1987.

Murphy, T. M., and Hardy, C. T. *Hospital–Physician Integration: Strategies for Success.* Chicago: American Hospital Publishing, 1994.

Additional Books of Interest

Hospital–Physician Integration:
Strategies for Success

by Terence M. Murphy and C. Thompson Hardy published in cooperation with the New England Healthcare Assembly

This book is a must-read for any hospital or physician group considering exploring integration options.

Hospital–Physician Integration provides an in-depth discussion of the major issues that are crucial to the process of integrating health care delivery systems. It focuses on the affiliation of existing organizations and presents the issues both through an analysis of the process as well as the presentation of seven detailed case studies.

Catalog No. E99-145159 (must be included when ordering)
1994. 237 pages, 54 figures, 12 tables. $57.50 (AHA members, $46.00)

Community Health Information Networks:
Creating the Health Care Data Highway

edited by Ralph T. Wakerly and First Consulting Group

Community Health Information Networks provides a starting point and reference work for executives and managers who are ready to act on the idea of a community health information network (CHIN). Based on the authors' practical experience in developing and managing a CHIN, rather than on theoretical ideas, this book shows readers how a CHIN provides an information network that supports a high-quality, cost-effective health care delivery system. The book focuses on the concepts, approaches, and trends in information technology that will have lasting value to readers. Divided into two parts, the book covers both the strategic issues of interest to senior executives and the practical hands-on information needed by the technical experts.

Catalog No. E99-093104 (must be included when ordering)
1994. 200 pages, 36 figures, 15 tables, glossary. $56.00 (AHA members, $45.00)

To order, call TOLL FREE 800-AHA-2626